CUPCAKE ENVY

AMY EILERT

CUPCAKE ENVY

IRRESISTIBLE CAKELETS—LITTLE CAKES THAT ARE FUN AND EASY

TUTTLE Publishing

Tokyo | Rutland, Vermont | Singapore

Contents

Foreword
by Norman R. Davis

Cupcake Envy features wonderful photography and clear, step-by-step instructions for constructing thirty-five amazing cakelets. Amy Eilert covers all the bases with mini cakes for young and old—perfect for a variety of occasions. Amy shows how to do it all—baking, shaping, icing, and decorating—in this fun and approachable guide. Amy conveys her know-how in such a simple, easy-to-understand manner that even novice cake decorators will enjoy this book and experience the satisfaction of creating fabulous single-serving cakes for friends and family.

Amy's insight and helpful tips will be of use to every cake artist. It's so easy to make these mini cakes your very own by applying your creativity to Amy's groundwork. Whether you are just starting to decorate or have years of experience, Amy's instructions will inspire you to bring these delightful mini cakes to life!

—Norman R. Davis, CMSA
(norman@thesweetlife.com), ICES Hall of Fame inductee and author of *Wedding Cake Ensembles*

Introduction
What Happens When You Think Outside the Wrapper

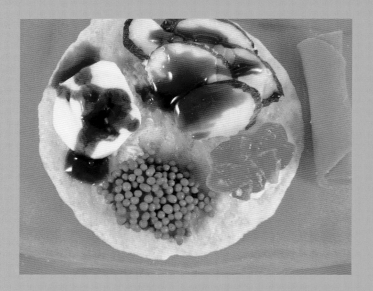

It was a Thursday afternoon and I was on my way to my son's preschool to help with the Jingle Bell Holiday Festival. My job was to bring the cupcakes. As I walked into the assembly room, I was overwhelmed by what I saw. There was Suzanne, scrap-booker extraordinaire, setting up an elaborate origami snowflake project. Near the teacher was Dana, handing out handmade snowman costumes for each child to wear during the sing-along portion of the festival.

It was obvious that the parent volunteers had spent countless hours on their contributions. And then there I was, like a deer in headlights, clinging to a container of store-bought cupcakes covered in florescent icing that was sure to stain every child's teeth (as well as Dana's handmade costumes). I felt defeated.

This was my life story when it came to desserts. I always wanted to create something special for office parties, holiday dinners, and neighborhood barbeques, but would inevitably succumb to confusion and intimidation and hit the grocery store bakery department instead.

Clearly, things had to change, so I rolled up my sleeves and faced my fears head on by putting myself in charge of desserts for my oldest son's kindergarten class. I was determined to make sweet, memorable treats that the kids, teachers, and parents would enjoy.

This time, I didn't waste hours worrying that my ideas might not work, or wait until the last minute before deciding it was too late to start. After putting my boys to bed, I spent a little time each night trying out different ideas using sprinkles and candies and whatever else I'd found in the baking aisle. I soon realized that decorating was the fun part—and the part that made the biggest impression.

I had decided to focus on cupcakes, because each child would get their own, thus avoiding tantrums over who got a bigger piece and who got the piece with the icing flower on top. I came up with a few really cool ideas and couldn't wait to try them out.

When my son brought home a school flyer for the annual Thanksgiving Feast Party, I knew this was my chance.

I made a batch of cupcakes and topped each one with a miniature, edible rendition of a traditional Thanksgiving dinner straight out of a Norman Rockwell painting. On the tiny dinner plate were turkey slices made from sliced almonds. Surrounding them were nonpareil "green peas," mashed potatoes made from a dollop of plain white icing, and cranberry relish made of chopped red gummy bears. I even impressed myself when I added some brown-tinted piping gel as a smooth, translucent gravy that pooled in the "mashed potatoes" and gently blanketed the "turkey slices."

I proudly brought my cupcakes to the school. The children loved them, but even more interesting were the reactions of the teachers and parents: They couldn't wipe the smiles off their faces. As I answered countless questions ("Did you make these all by yourself?" "How did you do it?" "How long did it take you?") it finally hit me: I didn't need a culinary degree or years of baking experience to make really cool, really delicious, and really impressive treats. I had what I needed all along.

From that moment on, the fire was lit. I went from messing with cupcakes and store-bought candies to creating a new kind of "cupcake"—mini cakes carved and decorated into fun three-dimensional designs. Before long, friends and neighbors had me creating all sorts of cakelets for birthdays, showers, and special occasions. People just couldn't get enough of these adorable, customized, personal-sized cakes.

That's when I launched Cupcake Envy, specializing in custom cakelets and coordinating cupcakes. When we figured out how to ship our cakelets, we quickly received orders from all over the country for cakelets in every design imaginable.

As impressive as cakelets look, the truth is anyone can make them. I'm proof that you don't need any baking skills or artistic talents to bring one to life. As you'll see in the following pages, all you need are a few tools and a lot of imagination to transform a single serving of cake into edible art.

Let's face it: There's only so much you can do to dress up a cupcake. But once you think outside the wrapper, the possibilities are endless—no experience required.

Chapter 1
Basic Tools and Ingredients

Those old sets of decorating tips for piping buttercream roses are just the tip of the iceberg. Today, you can walk into a craft store and find at least two full aisles of cake decorating tools, pans, and gadgets. So with all of the choices, how do you know what you need? Who even knows what to do with some of these fancy decorating tools and shimmer dusts? In this chapter, I will go over everything you need to make the cakelets in this book. I'll show you which decorating tools are must-haves, and how to use them.

BASIC PANS

You don't need to make a huge investment in tons of different pans to make the designs in this book. Most of the designs use standard cake pans you likely already have:

LOAF PANS (9 X 5-INCH) Cakes bake up narrower and taller, perfect for square shapes like dice and treasure chests.

MUFFIN TINS You can stack these to make tall figures like ghosts.

SQUARE 8 X 8-INCH AND RECTANGULAR 9 X 13-INCH CAKE PANS These are perfect for two-dimensional designs, such as T-shirts. Or you can stack layers to make designs that stand up, like purses and shopping bags.

Because many of my designs are carved out of a larger piece of cake, even if you don't have these pans you can still make a cakelet. Just find an oven-safe vessel (even a skillet will work) and bake a cake in it. Just try to pick a pan that will fit the cakelet design with as little waste as possible. By choosing the right pan, you can save batter for another project or for coordinating cupcakes.

SPECIALTY PANS

The baking industry has responded to the call for mini cakes by offering specialty pans in a wide variety of shapes. These are the most versatile and the ones I use most.

KING-SIZE MUFFIN PANS Perfect for coffee cups, tree stumps and giant cupcakes. Put two jumbo muffins together and you have a wine barrel.

9 X 13-INCH CAKE PAN

LOAF PAN

MINI WONDER MOLD

MINI BALL PAN

KING-SIZE MUFFIN PAN

MINI BALL PAN (SMALL HALF-BALLS) Great for creating sphere-shaped cakelets such as Christmas ornaments and sports balls.

MINI WONDER MOLD (MINI CONE-SHAPES) Great for dress bottoms, teacups, and igloos. Put two domes together and you have the makings of a Fabergé or Easter egg cakelet.

TIERED MINI CAKE PAN SETS These sets come in a variety of shapes—circles, squares, rectangles, octagons, and even topsy turvy. Since these sets usually come with three different sized pans, you can mix and match the shapes or use one of the pans for example, the rectangle pan to create the perfect shopping bag or suitcase cakelet.

TOOLS—THE NECESSITIES

Every project in this book requires this set of basic tools.

CORNSTARCH Used to keep your fondant from sticking to the mat when you roll it out, and it will keep your cutters from sticking, too. It's much whiter and finer than flour, which is not a good substitute.

FONDANT MODELING TOOL SET These sets typically consist of various sized ball tools used to thin out the edges of flower petals, as well as veiners which you poke into the middle of flowers to add realism. In addition to a standard set, you should add a quilting tool to create stitch marks on your fabric- and fashion-themed

BASIC FONDANT MODELING TOOL SET

PLASTIC WRAP AND WAXED PAPER

TAPERED ANGLED SPATULA

SERRATED KNIFE

SCISSORS

PASTRY WHEEL/ PIZZA WHEEL

CUP OF WATER

X-ACTO KNIFE

CORNSTARCH

PAINT BRUSH

PLACEMAT

ROLLING PIN

designs. You will also need a double-sided flower veiner to create a realistic flower petal texture to both sides of a fondant flower cut out.

GEL FOOD COLORING Think of these like an artist's paints. They come in an amazing array of shades, are more intense than liquid food coloring, and can be blended to make custom colors. I prefer those in soft plastic squeeze bottles so I can add a drop of color at a time.

PARCHMENT OR WAXED PAPER Essential for keeping your work surface free of stray crumbs and buttercream.

PASTRY WHEEL/PIZZA WHEEL Pastry or pizza wheels make it easy to make precise cuts along a straight line or around the bottom of a cakelet. The best pastry wheels also include a scalloped blade, for those times when you need a scalloped edge to your fondant.

PLACEMAT You are going to need a smooth, nonstick surface for rolling out fondant. Although many people use Silpat mats, they're expensive and easy to damage when cutting out shapes with an X-Acto knife. Cheap placemats from a dollar store are a great option because they're affordable, easy to replace, and can withstand the X-Acto blade rather well.

PLASTIC WRAP To keep cakes and fondant from drying out before you work with them, you'll need to wrap them in plastic.

ROLLING PIN Rolling pins come in various sizes, weights and materials. You can even get bands to put on them to help you roll out your dough or fondant to a precise thickness. They can get pricey, so if you're looking to save a little money, or want to add a small or medium roller to your collection for rolling out tiny bits of fondant, head over to your home improvement store and ask an employee to cut a short length of PVC pipe. Sand both ends smooth, run it through the dishwasher and you have yourself a rolling pin!

SCISSORS Don't use your kids' art scissors or that rusty pair from the junk drawer. Every kitchen should have a dedicated, sharp, food-safe pair of scissors on hand.

SERRATED KNIFE A serrated edge cuts through cake without squashing or flattening it.

SPATULA When working with cakelets, I prefer a tapered angled spatula. I prefer the Ateco brand because the metal is very thin and flexible making it easy to ice contoured cake shapes.

WATER AND PAINT BRUSH These are essential for adhering fondant pieces to each other.

X-ACTO KNIFE Commonly found in art supply stores and hardware stores, X-Acto knives are essential for making detailed, precise cuts.

REVITALIZE DRYING FONDANT WITH A SMALL AMOUNT OF SHORTENING APPLIED TO THE SURFACE.

SHORTENING When working on fondant decorations, you may find that your fondant is drying too quickly, causing it to tear and wrinkle. Just put a little bit of shortening on your finger and work it into the fondant to make it workable again.

OTHER ESSENTIALS

EMBOSSING ROLLERS Easily add beautiful patterns and dimensional textures to fondant with these handy tools.

FONDANT CUTTERS There is a wide variety of cutters out there, including flowers, geometric shapes, damask patterns, themed sets, and funky shapes. Don't limit yourself to the cutters in your local craft store. Online cake decorating stores offer an amazing selection of cutters, and eBay is a great source of cutters not available in the U.S. Consider buying a craft organizer for storage.

FONDANT SMOOTHERS Although you can smooth fondant over a cakelet with your hands, a fondant smoother will help you make perfect edges and super-flat surfaces. They're also useful for making perfectly rounded and smooth handles for purses and shopping bags.

IMPRESSION MATS These textured plastic sheets are used to press an embossed pattern into a sheet of fondant. They come in a huge variety of patterns, from bricks and stones, to swirls, stripes, and laces.

LETTER PRESSES Adding a monogram or name is a great way to personalize a cakelet, and letter presses ensure it'll look slick and professional. Although there are letter and number cutters known as Tapits, they're not always user friendly. Instead, I use letter presses designed for clay projects. They are easy to use, affordable, and commonly found in most craft stores.

MOLDS Using molds makes your cake look like a pro's. Simply push a ball of fondant into a silicone mold and you get an edible design or figure that would take ages to create by hand. Molds can be expensive, so shop around and try to pick a mold that you'll find multiple uses for.

PIPING BAGS Use piping bags to place a neat bead of frosting or royal icing precisely where you want it. They are great for adding fine details or lettering. The bags are available in many different varieties including silicone, reusable

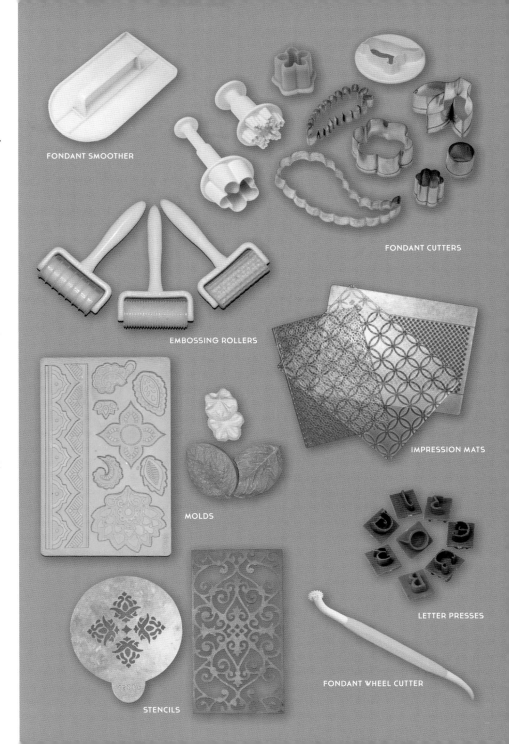

FONDANT SMOOTHER

FONDANT CUTTERS

EMBOSSING ROLLERS

IMPRESSION MATS

MOLDS

LETTER PRESSES

FONDANT WHEEL CUTTER

STENCILS

cotton, parchment assembled, and plastic disposables.

STENCILS Even if you have no artistic ability, you can use a stencil to add intricate decorations to your cakes. Just place the stencil on top of the fondant, then use a spatula to spread royal icing over the stenciled pattern. Remove any excess icing and gently peel away the stencil. That's it!

DUSTS

Dusts are a great way to add shading for flowers, contour to sculpted shapes, and a shimmer or a metallic shine. They come in dozens of colors. When choosing which one to use, try to match it closely to the color of the fondant. There are three main types that I use:

DISCO DUST Edible glitter! That's the best way to describe this relatively new kind of dust.

LUSTER DUSTS These are like eye shadow. They add a shimmery, luster effect to your fondant. When mixed with vodka, they turn into metallic paint.

PETAL DUSTS These dusts add a matte finish, which is great for adding depth and shading to your designs. And if you're interested in hand painting on fondant, petal dust is the way to go. Just mix it with vodka.

INGREDIENTS

There have been many times when I've been in the middle of a cake design when I suddenly realize I don't have exactly what I need. Over the years, I've been able to improvise and have found that there are plenty of ingredients commonly found in your local grocery store that will do just fine.

CAKE Since cakelets are small, there is no need for complex support systems or ultra-firm cakes. Almost any recipe (except angel food) will work, including box cake mixes.

FONDANT There was a time when fondant had a bad rap—it didn't taste good and it was hard to find. Thankfully that's not the case today because it's so much fun to work with. Every design in this book relies on fondant. You can buy delicious fondant online or in craft stores in a rainbow of colors.

DISCO DUST   LUSTER DUST   PETAL DUST

Chapter 2
Tricks of the Trade

Bake, chill, carve, and decorate. That's all it takes to make the cakelets in this book. Admittedly, decorating takes the most effort, but it's also the best part. Here are a few of my tricks to make things even easier.

TIPS

COLD CAKES ARE EASIER TO CARVE
The key to making cakelets easy to carve and decorate is to always work with a chilled cake. They're firmer and they lose fewer crumbs. But that means you need to plan ahead and give your fully cooled cake time to chill in the freezer for a couple hours. If you try to carve a cake that is room temperature, it may start to fall apart—and then so will you. Nobody needs that kind of stress!

TEMPLATES MAKE IT EASY
Templates are great tools as they take the guesswork out of carving your cake into a cakelet. Place the template over the cake and cut around it using a serrated steak knife (since the cakes are small, there's no need for a big bread knife). Use the template as a guide to cut around the shape. I've provided several templates at the end of this book. But you can also create your own templates to create cakelets of your own design.

THICK CAKES ARE TASTIER WITH FILLING
I create some of the taller designs by stacking pieces of cake with layers of frosting in the middle, so they're more delicious. But this can be tricky with some designs. That's when I use loaf pans so

I have a big firm chunk of cake to work with. To keep the cake portion from being overwhelming when eaten, simply core out a few holes in the bottom of the cake before decorating, then fill in the holes with your favorite icings or fillings.

WORKING WITH COLORED DUSTS
In general, choose a shade slightly darker than the fondant. Luster dust adds shimmer while petal dust adds the appearance of depth, and both go on best with puffy brushes, which you can find at art stores. To use, tap some dust from the jar onto a plate, dab your brush in the dust, tap the handle to allow the excess to fall off, then brush over your design.

While luster dusts are generally brushed over a large area of fondant to give it shine, petal dusts are more often

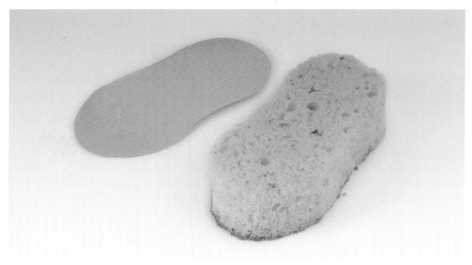

used on smaller, more concentrated areas to add depth. For example, if I am making light pink flowers and would like to add a more realistic effect, I dab a darker shade of pink petal dust from the center of the flower outward. If I am making a brown doggie cakelet, I would use a darker brown dust around the eyes, mouth and legs to add dimension.

If you want to paint on fondant, dusts are the way to go. Just mix them with vodka. Don't mix dusts with water, since the water won't dry and will instead leave your fondant feeling tacky to the touch. Luster dust makes metallic paint, which is great for accents and jewelry, while petal dust makes more traditional paint. The less vodka you use, the more opaque the paint is. Add a little more vodka and you will have a more translucent painting stroke.

Since disco dust is essentially edible glitter, paint the fondant with vodka, then shake the dust over it while it's still wet. A word of caution: After using it, you will be find remnants of disco dust for a few days no matter how thoroughly you clean up!

TINTING FONDANT

It's easy to tint fondant. The trick is to start with a small amount of gel color and knead it in completely before deciding if you need more to reach the desired shade. You might be surprised by how effective just a few drops can be once they're completely incorporated into the fondant.

To avoid staining your hands, be sure to use food-service gloves. Warm the fondant by kneading it until it's pliable. Add a few dots of gel color to the surface in several spots, then knead the color into the ball until it's evenly distributed. Add more dots of color if necessary. Dark colors—such as black, brown, and red—typically need more applications of gel color, even up to one full ounce (25 ml). Keep any fondant sealed in an airtight container until you're ready to use it.

USING A PIPING BAG

Piping bags are available in many different varieties. Preparation is simple if you're using plastic disposable piping bags. If using only one decorating tip, simply cut off the bottom point of the bag just enough so that the design of the tip is exposed. If you cut away too much, the tip will fall through the bag or icing can leak out of the sides of the opening.

If you want to use multiple tips for the same piping bag, you will need a coupler. Couplers consist of a base and a ring. First, cut a hole big enough for the bottom half of the base to be exposed. Pull the bag tight so that the base is firmly in place. Next, place a tip onto the exposed coupler base and tighten it in place with the ring. That way, all you will have to do is unscrew the ring to change out your decorating tips.

After your decorating tip is in place, fill the bag with icing. Open it up and fold the top part of the bag over the hand that is holding the bag. Now you can easily fill the bag without getting icing on your hands. Unfold the bag from your hands and give the bag a twist so that icing does not leak out of the top. If you are working with kids, simply use string to tie the top of the bag tight so that they will not have icing leaking out of the top. Place the twisted part of the bag between the base of your thumb and index finger. Press your thumb to your index finger and begin piping. Use all four fingers to squeeze the bag. Be sure to practice using the appropriate amount of pressure for your decorating.

BASIC RECIPES

VERSATILE VANILLA CAKE
MAKES 4 CUPS OF BATTER

This moist, tender cake is easy make and uses staples you likely have on hand. It bakes up beautifully no matter what type of cake pan you use. Vanilla bean paste gives the cake the best flavor. The paste's popularity is rising among bakers, making it easier to find at better grocery stores. It's also widely available online.

½ cup (115 g) unsalted butter, at room temperature

1 cup (200 g) granulated sugar

2 large eggs, at room temperature

2 teaspoons pure vanilla bean paste (or 2 teaspoons vanilla extract)

1½ cups (215 g) all-purpose flour

1¾ teaspoons (8 ml) baking powder

½ cup (125 ml) whole milk, at room temperature

Preheat oven to 350°F (180°C). Spray cake pan with nonstick spray, sprinkle with flour and tap out the excess.

In the bowl of a stand mixer fitted with the paddle attachment, cream the butter and sugar together on high speed until light and fluffy, about 6 minutes (stop and scrape down the sides of the bowl once or twice). With the mixer on medium speed, add the eggs, one at a time, beating the first one until completely incorporated before adding the next. Beat in the vanilla paste (or extract, if using).

In a medium bowl, whisk together the flour and baking powder. With the mixer on low speed, add the dry ingredients to the butter mixture, alternating with the milk. Pour or spoon batter into the prepared pan

---

BAKING TIMES BY PAN

Brownie pan (9 x 6 in; 23 x 15 cm or 8-in/20.5-cm square)—
20 to 30 minutes

Wilton Mini Wonder Mold Pan—
approximately 20 minutes

Wilton King-Size Muffin Pan—
approximately 25 minutes

Wilton Mini Ball pan—
approximately 15 minutes

9 x 5-in (23 x 12.5-cm) **loaf pan**—
30 to 35 minutes

9 x 13-in (23 x 33-cm) **cake pan**—
30 to 40 minutes

---

and bake according to the chart above. The cake is done when a toothpick inserted into the center comes out clean and the top springs back when lightly touched.

ROYAL ICING
MAKES 3 CUPS

Royal icing is perfect for writing names and adding delicate designs to your cakelets because it's easy to pipe and dries hard, so there's no risk of smudging. You can tint it with gel food coloring, as well. For making outlines and names, be sure the icing is relatively stiff. If you want to fill in an area with icing (the technical term is "flooding"), thin it out a little with more water. Meringue powder can be found in the cake decorating aisle at craft stores.

4 cups (450 g) powdered sugar

2 tablespoons meringue powder

6 tablespoons water

In the bowl of a standing mixer fitted with the whisk attachment, beat the all the ingredients together on low speed for 7 to 10 minutes, or until the icing loses its shine (stop to scrape down the sides of the bowl several times). Add more water by the teaspoon if the icing appears too stiff to pipe easily. Store icing in an air-tight container at room temperature.

VANILLA FROSTING
MAKES 3 CUPS

What I love about this frosting is how easy it is to work with. Vegetable shortening-based frosting keeps longer and resists melting better than butter-based frostings and results in a pure-white color that is easier to tint.

1 cup (191 g) vegetable shortening

1 tablespoon (15 g) meringue powder

1 teaspoon (5 ml) pure vanilla bean paste (or 1 teaspoon vanilla extract)

2 tablespoons plus 1½ teaspoons (35 ml) water

1 lb (454 g) confectioner's sugar

In the bowl of a standing mixer fitted with the paddle attachment, combine all ingredients. Place a damp kitchen towel over the mixer to keep the powdered sugar from billowing out. Turn the mixer on low and gradually increase the speed to medium-high as the ingredients come together. Beat until light and fluffy. Store icing in an air-tight container at room temperature.

Chapter 3

Fun, Flirty and Fabulous

In the Bag

The purse cakelet is always a big hit in my classes because it offers endless decorating possibilities. You can make it dainty, sophisticated, trendy, or whimsical. You can add flowers, polka dots, or even recreate a famous designer's insignia. It's so easy to customize for the lucky recipient. Just consider her favorite colors and sense of style, then let your imagination go.

Tools

9 x 6-in (23 x 15-cm) metal brownie pan
The Necessities (pages 11–12)
Purse template (see Templates, page 115)
Flower cutter set
Texture sheet

Ingredients

One 16-oz (455-g) box cake mix (any flavor) prepared, or batter for one 9-in (23-cm) cake
1 recipe Vanilla Frosting (page 17) or 1 container store-bought frosting
12 oz (340 g) white fondant (see Resources, page 114)
Red gel food coloring (or other accent color)
Yellow gel food coloring (or other base color)

Prepare the handle (two days prior to decorating)

1 Tint 11 oz (310 g) of the fondant with the yellow gel food coloring (or other base color of your choice).

2 Roll out 1 oz (28 g) of the base-color fondant into a curved, rounded strip to create the purse handle. Place on a piece of parchment paper and set aside to dry for at least two days at room temperature out of direct sunlight (to keep the color from fading). Wrap the remaining base-color fondant in plastic wrap until ready to use.

Bake the cake

1 Preheat oven to 350°F (180°C). Prepare the cake batter. Spray the brownie pan with non-stick spray.

2 Pour the batter into the pan, filling it three-quarters full. Smooth the top and bake for 20–30 minutes, or until the top springs back when lightly pressed and a toothpick inserted into the center comes out clean.

3 Place the pan on a wire rack to cool for about 10 minutes. If the cake rose above the pan, use a serrated knife to cut away the top of the cake to make it level (set the knife across the top of the pan so you can use it as a guide). Run a knife around the edge to loosen the sides. Invert the cake out of the pan onto a wire rack and allow it to finish cooling. When completely cool, wrap in plastic wrap and freeze for at least two hours until cold and firm.

Prepare to decorate

1 Remove the cake from the freezer and unwrap it atop a piece of parchment paper. Cut the cake in half. Apply a layer of Vanilla Frosting to one half and stack the other half on top.

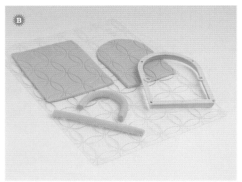

Level *Easy/Intermediate*
Batter yields enough cake for *1 cakelet*
Fondant quantity listed is suitable to complete *1 cakelet*

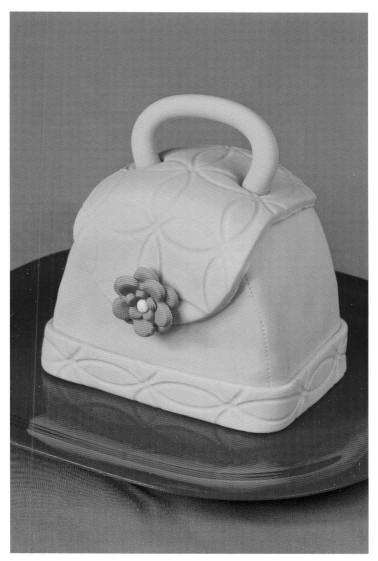

2 Place the Purse template against the cake and use a sharp knife to cut out the cake, using the template as a guide. Use the knife to clean up any rough edges of the cakelet. ☀

3 Using a tapered angled spatula, crumb coat the cakelet with Vanilla Frosting, starting around the sides of the cake and finishing on the top. Use enough frosting so that the spatula doesn't come into direct contact with the cake. This will keep you from dislodging too many crumbs.

Cover the cakelet

1 Dust a clean, dry work surface with cornstarch. Roll out 6 oz (170 g) of base-color fondant into a $\frac{1}{4}$ in (6 mm) thick circle.

2 Slide your hands underneath the fondant using open palms so as not to poke a hole in it. Pick it up and lay it over the cakelet. Smooth the top first, using an open palm. Then smooth the fondant down over the sides. Use the pastry wheel to cut away excess fondant around the bottom of the cakelet.

3 Roll out the remaining base-color fondant into a $\frac{1}{4}$ in (6 mm) thick sheet. Use the Purse template to cut out a flap. Re-roll the fondant scraps and cut out a $\frac{3}{4}$ in (1.8 cm) wide by 12 in (30.5 cm) long strip for the bottom border of the purse.

Finishing touches

Set the texture sheet you prefer onto the fondant flap and border and press it in to make the indented pattern. ☀ Use a paintbrush to dab a little water where you want to adhere the border and gently press it into place. Repeat with the flap.

Embellishments: Tint the remaining white fondant into a contrasting color (or several colors) to use for embellishments. Consider making a flower, bow or a plaque with a monogram for the front of the flap. ☀ Use a paintbrush and water to adhere them.

Handle: Gently press the dry handle into the top of the purse to make a mark where you want it to go. Use a ball tool to push down into the marked areas to make holes, which will make it easier to insert the handle. (If you don't do this step and simply push your handle in, you risk breaking it.)

Breakfast at Tiffany's

Who doesn't love a little retail therapy? Anyone who lives for hitting the malls or who is always decked out in the latest styles will love this cakelet. The design is simple to create and you can customize the bag with your favorite store names, or the monogram of the recipient. Don't be afraid to get creative and have fun with it!

Tools
The Necessities (pages 11–12)
9 x 6-in (23 x 15-cm) metal brownie pan
Small and medium flower cutters (see Resources, page 114)

Ingredients
One 16-oz (455-g) box cake mix (any flavor) prepared, or batter for one 9-in (23-cm) cake
1 recipe Vanilla Frosting (page 17) or 1 container store-bought frosting
1½ lbs (680 g) white fondant (see Resources, page 114)
Blue gel food coloring

Make the handles (two days prior to decorating)
1 Dust a clean, dry work surface with cornstarch. Using a fondant smoother, roll out two 4-oz (115-g) pieces of white fondant into two logs 6 in (15 cm) long and ¼ in (6 mm) thick. Bend each log into the shape of a "U." ✱

2 Place handles on a piece of parchment paper and set them aside to dry out for at least two days at room temperature out of direct sunlight (to keep the color from fading).

Bake the cake
1 Preheat oven to 350°F (180°C). Prepare the cake batter. Spray the brownie pan with non-stick spray.

2 Pour the batter into the pan, filling it three-quarters full. Smooth the top and bake for 20 to 30 minutes, or until the top springs back when lightly pressed and a toothpick inserted into the center comes out clean.

3 Place the pan on a wire rack to cool for about 10 minutes. If the cake rose above the pan, use a serrated knife to cut away the top of the cake to make it level (set the knife across the top of the pan so you can use it as a guide). Run a knife around the edge to loosen the sides. Invert the cake out of the pan onto a wire rack and allow it to finish cooling. When completely cool, wrap in plastic wrap and freeze for at least two hours until cold and firm.

Prepare to decorate
1 Remove cake from the freezer and unwrap. Use a serrated knife to cut out a 4½ x 3¼-in (11.25 x 8.1-cm) rectangle. 🅱 Place upright on a piece of parchment.

2 Using a tapered angled spatula, crumb coat the four sides of the cakelet (but not the top or bottom) with the Vanilla Frosting. Use enough frosting so that the spatula doesn't come into

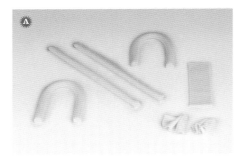

direct contact with the cake. This will keep you from dislodging too many crumbs.

Cover the cakelet
1 Tint ¾ lb (340 g) of the fondant with the blue gel food color. Dust a clean, dry work surface with cornstarch. Roll out the fondant into a sheet ¼ in (6 mm) thick and about 10 in (25.5 cm) long and 5 in (12.5 cm) wide.

2 Set the iced cake onto the fondant, allowing for an extra fondant lip at the top. (You

Level *Easy/Intermediate*
Batter yields enough cake for *1 cakelet*
Fondant quantity listed is suitable to complete *1 cakelet*

want the fondant to be a little higher than the cake to give the impression of a bag and so you can add the fondant tissue paper effect coming out of the top.) Gently wrap the fondant around the cake and cut away any excess. Your fondant seam should be in the back corners of the cake. Smooth with palms or a fondant smoother.

3 Once the cake is completely wrapped, stand the cake upright onto a piece of parchment.

4 To make the bag creases, use the scoring tool to score a triangle at the bottom of each side of the bag. Starting at the top of the triangle, score a straight line up to the top of the bag.

Assemble

1 Use the blue gel food coloring to tint approximately 4 oz (115 g) of fondant a lighter or darker shade of blue to complement the bag. (You can divide the fondant in half and tint it two different shades, or chose a different color altogether—or opt to use none at all: I went with white in the example to the right). Roll the fondant out into a thin sheet. Use a pastry wheel to cut randomly-shaped pieces from it. This will be your "tissue paper."

2 Apply frosting onto the top inside edge of the bag and use it to adhere the pieces of "tissue." For a more realistic look, fold some pieces over the top of the bag.

3 Very gently press the dried handles into the "tissue" to make a mark where you want the handles to go. Use a ball tool to push down into the marked areas to make a hole, which will make it easier to insert the handles. (If you don't do this step and simply push your handles into the tissue, you will risk breaking the handles...trust me!)

Finishing touches

Roll out the remaining white fondant into a sheet $\frac{1}{8}$ in (3 mm) thick. Cut out several 4 in (10 cm) long strips that are $\frac{3}{4}$ in wide (1.8 cm). Use a little water to adhere the white fondant stripes vertically around the entire shopping bag.

Decorating ideas

Roll out fondant and use cutters or pattern tools to create embellishments for decorating the bag. Some ideas include: flowers, paisley motifs, store names, monograms, and patterns or stripes.

Flower Party

Sometimes even a cakelet is bigger than you need. When just a bite or two will do, this mini-cakelet is the perfect solution. It's decorated with delicate flowers—a simple, versatile, customizable design that works for almost any situation, from tea parties to wedding favors.

Tools
9 x 13-in (23 x 33-cm) cake pan
The Necessities (pages 11–12)
3-in (7.5-cm) circle cutter
Medium blossom cutter
Toothpick

Ingredients
One 16-oz (455-g) box cake mix (any flavor) prepared, or batter for one 9-in (23-cm) cake
1 recipe Vanilla Frosting (page 17) or 1 container store-bought frosting
1 lb (455 g) white fondant (see Resources, page 114)
Red gel food coloring
Pink gel food coloring

Bake the cake
1 Preheat oven to 350°F (180°C). Prepare the cake batter. Spray the cake pan with non-stick spray.

2 Pour the batter into the pan, filling it three-quarters full. Smooth the top and bake for 25 minutes, or until the top springs back when lightly pressed and a toothpick inserted into the center comes out clean.

3 Place the pan on a wire rack to cool for about 10 minutes. If the cake rose above the pan, use a serrated knife to cut away the top

of the cake to make it level (set the knife across the top of the pan so you can use it as a guide). Run a knife around the edge to loosen the sides. Invert the cake out of the pan onto a wire rack and allow it to finish cooling. When completely cool, wrap in plastic wrap and freeze for at least two hours until cold and firm.

Prepare to decorate
1 Use the pink food coloring to tint 4 oz (115 g) of the fondant the desired shade of light pink. Use the red food coloring to tint 5 oz (140 g) of the fondant the desired shade of dark pink. Wrap in plastic wrap until ready to use.

2 Remove the cake from the freezer and unwrap. Use the 3-in (7.5-cm) circle cutter to cut the cake into up to eight round mini cakes (you will need two mini cakes for one cakelet).

3 Coat the top of a mini cake with Vanilla Frosting. Stack another cake on top of it to create a layered mini cakelet about 3 in (7.5 cm) high.

4 Place the cakelet on a piece of parchment. Using a tapered angled spatula, crumb coat the cakelet with Vanilla Frosting, starting at the sides and finishing

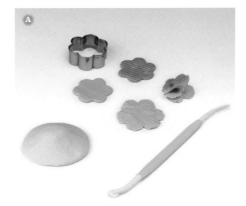

at the top. Use enough frosting so that the spatula doesn't come into direct contact with the cake. This will keep you from dislodging too many crumbs.

Cover the mini cakelet
1 Dust a clean, dry work surface with cornstarch. Roll out 6 oz (170 g) of the white fondant into a circle $\frac{1}{4}$ in (6 mm) thick and 9 in (23 cm) in diameter.

2 Slide your hands under the fondant, lift up and lay it on top of the mini cakelet.

3 Use two fondant smoothers to smooth the top and sides of the cake. Cut away excess fondant around the base with a pastry wheel.

4 Place in the refrigerator to chill for 30 minutes.

Level *Easy*
Batter yields enough cake for *4 mini cakelets*
Fondant quantity listed is suitable to complete *1 mini cakelet*

Finishing touches

1 Dust a clean, dry work surface with cornstarch. Roll out 1 oz (28 g) of the white fondant into a 2-in (5-cm) ball. Flatten the bottom of the ball and use a little water to adhere it to the top of the mini-cakelet.

2 Roll out 4 oz (115 g) of the light-shaded pink fondant into a sheet $\frac{1}{8}$ in (3 mm) thick. Use the medium blossom cutter to cut out approximately thirty blossoms. ✴

3 Roll out 3 oz (85 g) of the darker shaded pink fondant into a sheet $\frac{1}{8}$ in (3 mm) thick. Use the medium blossom cutter to cut out approximately twenty blossoms.

4 Use the ball tool to thin the edges of the petals. Loosely fold the flower in half, and then in half again. Spread the petals out a bit.

5 Brush the entire white ball with water. Use a veining tool to insert blossoms into it. You want the entire ball to be covered and appear lush, which is why it requires a lot of blossoms. Be sure to have a nice mixture of light shaded and dark shaded blossoms on the mini-cakelet.

6 Roll out 2 oz (55 g) of the darker shade of pink fondant into a strip approximately $\frac{1}{8}$ in (3 mm) thick, 9 in (23 cm) long, and $\frac{3}{4}$ in (1.8 cm) wide.

7 Adhere the pink fondant strip around the base of the mini-cakelet using water and a paintbrush.

Fun, Flirty and Fabulous **25**

Playing Dress-Up

Level *Easy/Intermediate*
Batter yields enough cake for *4 cakelets*
Fondant quantity listed is suitable
to complete *1 cakelet*

Is there anything more fabulous than a beautiful dress custom-made just for you? How about one you don't have to worry about fitting into? This is one of the first cakelet designs I created for my business, Cupcake Envy. It started out pretty simple, but over the years I've had a lot of fun changing the style, pattern, and adding sweet and stylish accents. It's so easy to mix things up that it's hard to know when to stop. Now, there are so many dress designs in my repertoire I can practically create my own fashion label. Just watch: once you make your first dress you won't be able to resist playing dress-up, too.

Tools

4-cavity mini dome baking pan
The Necessities (pages 11–12)
Templates for Dress Top, Skirt Panel, and
**   optional Hanger (see Templates, page 115)**
Small and medium flower cutters
Flower veiner tool
Piping bag with #2 cake decorating tip
Paring knife

Ingredients

One 16-oz (455-g) box cake mix (any flavor)
**   prepared, or batter for one 9-in (23-cm) cake**
1 recipe Vanilla Frosting (page 17) or 1
**   container store-bought frosting**
1 lb (455 g) white fondant
**   (see Resources, page 114)**
1 recipe Royal Icing (page 17)
Three shades of gel food coloring (a base color,
**   a complementary color, and an accent color)**

Prepare to decorate

Color 6½ oz (185 g) of fondant using the gel food coloring for the desired base color of the dress. (See tinting instructions on page 16). Color 7½ oz (210 g) of fondant with a contrasting but complementary color for the skirt, waistline, and optional neckline. Color 1 oz (28 g) of fondant a strong accent color for the center of the waistline and the corsage. Wrap each color separately in plastic wrap or a zip top bag until ready to use.

Make the dress top (two days prior to decorating)

1 Dust a clean, dry work surface with cornstarch. Roll out 2½ oz (70 g) of the base color fondant to ⅛ in (3 mm) thick. If you want to embellish the dress top by pressing it with a texture sheet, do it now.

2 Place the Dress Top template on the fondant. Use an X-Acto knife to cut out the form using the template as a guide. Place the dress top on a piece of parchment paper

and set aside to dry for 2–3 days at room temperature out of direct sunlight (to keep the color from fading).

Make the hangers (optional)

1 Attach a #2 cake decorating tip to a piping bag. Fill the bag with white royal icing.

2 Use the Hanger template to trace 3–10 hanger shapes onto a piece of parchment paper (the extras are in case of breakage). Flip the paper (you should still be able to see the lines you drew) and pipe the icing along the lines. Allow to dry for 24 hours. Keep your extra hangers for future dress projects in a Tupperware container for up to six months.

Bake the cake

1 Preheat oven to 350°F (180°C). Spray each of the mini dome pan cavities to be used with non-stick spray (you will need one mini dome cake for one cakelet). Fill each cavity being used three-quarters full with batter. Bake for 15 to 20 minutes, or until the top springs back when lightly pressed and a toothpick inserted into the center comes out clean.

2 Allow cake to cool for a few minutes in the pan. If the cake rose above the pan, use a serrated knife to cut away the top to make it level (set the knife across the top of the pan so you can use it as a guide). Run a knife around the edge to loosen the sides. Invert the cake out of the pan and place it on a wire rack to finish cooling. When completely cool, wrap in plastic wrap and freeze for at least two hours until cold and firm.

Prepare the skirt

1 Place the mini dome cake on a square piece of parchment paper. Using a tapered angled spatula, apply a smooth crumb coat of Vanilla Frosting over the cake. Use enough frosting so that the spatula doesn't come into direct contact with the cake. This will keep you from dislodging too many crumbs.

2 Dust your work surface with cornstarch. Roll out $5\frac{1}{2}$ oz (160 g) of complementary-color fondant (I used white on the dress shown on the page 26) to an 8-in (20.5-cm) circle that's $\frac{1}{4}$ in (6 mm) thick.

3 Slide your hands underneath the fondant using open palms so as not to poke a hole in it. Pick the fondant up and gently lay it over the mini cake and smooth it down. Alternatively, you could allow the folds to naturally drape, which gives the impression of draped fabric. Use your pastry wheel to cut away excess fondant around the bottom of the dress.

Assemble

1 Using the dried dress top, gently press an indentation into the top of the fondant-covered cake to give yourself a guideline for cutting.

2 Using a paring knife, cut through the fondant along the indention. Insert the dress top.

3 Dust your work surface with cornstarch. Roll out 4 oz (115 g) of base-color fondant into a sheet $\frac{1}{8}$ in (3 mm) thick. Place the Skirt Panel template on the fondant. Use an X-Acto knife to cut out eight triangular panels, using the template as a guide. Brush the panels with a little water and press lightly to apply the triangles at regular intervals around the skirt.

4 Dust a work surface with cornstarch. Roll out 2 oz (55 g) of the complementary-color fondant until it is $\frac{1}{4}$ in (6 mm) thick. Cut out a strip that is 4 in (10 cm) long and $\frac{1}{2}$ in (1.25 cm) wide to make a waistband, and a strip that is 2 in (5 cm) long and $\frac{1}{2}$ in (1.25 cm) wide to make a neckline (optional).

corsage). Optionally, cut an additional 15–20 flowers per dress with the small flower cutter to form a floral hem.

2 If creating a hem, brush the bottom of edge of the skirt with a little water. Arrange a row of small flowers along the bottom of the skirt. Using the veining tool (page 11), poke the tip of the veiner into each flower, pressing the flower into the bottom of the dress. This will result in a seamless flower border around the bottom of the dress.

3 To add a flower corsage, dab the dress top with a little water where you want to place the corsage. Press a medium flower onto the area with your fingers. Dab the flower with a little water and place a center a small flower on top.

4 Use the piping bag filled with royal icing tinted to match the accent color and fitted with a #2 tip to pipe flourishes around each flower. Optionally, pipe several decorative dots on the waist band.

5 To adhere the optional hanger to the dress, apply a dot of royal icing on the back of each shoulder on the back of the dress. Press the bottom of the hanger to it and hold for a few seconds. See page 113 for an example of a dress with the optional floral hem and hanger in place.

5 Roll out 1 oz (28 g) of accent color fondant until $\frac{1}{4}$ in (6 mm) thick. Cut out a strip that is 4 in (10 cm) long and $\frac{1}{4}$ in (6 mm) wide to complete the waistband. Cut out another strip that is 2 in (5 cm) long and $\frac{1}{4}$ in (6 mm) wide to complete the neckline, if using.

6 Brush the contrasting-colored fondant strips with a little water. Center the corresponding accent-color fondant strips on top, pressing lightly to adhere.

7 Using the paint brush, apply a little water around the base of the dress top. Wrap the waistband around the base of the dress top with the seam in the back. Repeat with the optional neckline strip.

Finishing touches

1 Dust a work surface with cornstarch. Roll out the remaining accent color fondant until it is $\frac{1}{8}$ in (3 mm) thick. Use the medium flower cutter to cut out one flower per dress (for the

Favorite T-Shirt

Everyone has a favorite T-shirt. You know the one. It's well-worn and soft, and the first thing you put on right out of the dryer. With this cakelet, you can pay homage to your piece of 100-percent cotton comfort, or unleash your inner clothing designer and create something totally new.

Tools

The Necessities (pages 11–12)
9 x 13-in (23 x 33-cm) cake pan
T-Shirt template (see Templates, page 115)
Bird cutter (if using—see Resources, page 114)
Stitching tool (see Resources, page 114)

Ingredients

One 16-oz (455-g) box cake mix (any flavor) prepared, or batter for one 9-in (23-cm) cake
1 recipe Vanilla Frosting (page 17) or 1 container store-bought frosting
8 oz (225 g) white fondant (see Resources, page 114)
Blue gel food coloring
1 oz (30 g) chocolate fondant, brown colored fondant, or 3 mini Tootsie Rolls

Bake the cake

1 Preheat oven to 350°F (180°C). Prepare the cake batter. Spray the pan with non-stick spray.

2 Pour the batter into the pan, filling it three-quarters full. Smooth the top and bake for 30–40 minutes, or until the top springs back when lightly pressed and a toothpick inserted into the center comes out clean.

3 Place pan on a wire rack to cool for about 10 minutes. If the cake rose above the pan, use a serrated knife to cut away the top of the cake to make it level (set the knife across the top of the pan so you can use it as a guide). Run a knife around the edge to loosen the sides. Invert the cake out of the pan onto a wire rack and allow to finish cooling. When completely cool, wrap in plastic wrap and freeze for at least two hours until cold and firm.

Prepare to decorate

1 If recreating the pictured design, use the blue gel food coloring to tint 1 oz (30 g) of the white fondant (see tinting instructions on page 16). Wrap tightly with plastic wrap until ready to use.

2 Remove cake from the freezer and unwrap. Place the T-shirt template on top of the cake and use a sharp knife to cut out the cake around it. ✽ Remove template and use the knife to clean up any rough edges.

3 Place the cakelet on a piece of parchment. Using a tapered angled spatula, crumb coat the cakelet with Vanilla Frosting starting around the sides of the cake and finishing on the top. Use enough frosting so that the spatula doesn't come into direct contact with the cake. This will keep you from dislodging too many crumbs. (If you find that the cake has thawed and is difficult to coat, rewrap and place in the refrigerator or freezer until firm again.)

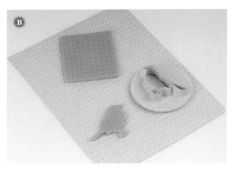

Cover the cakelet

1 Dust a clean, dry work surface with cornstarch. Roll out 6 oz (170 g) of the white fondant into a sheet $\frac{1}{4}$ in (6 mm) thick and large enough to cover the cakelet.

Level *Easy*
Batter yields enough cake for *4 cakelets*
Fondant quantity listed is suitable to complete *1 cakelet*

2 Slide your hands underneath the fondant using open palms so as not to poke a hole in it. Pick it up and lay the fondant over the cakelet. Smooth the top first, using an open palm. Then smooth the fondant down over the sides.

3 Use a pastry wheel to cut away excess fondant around the bottom of the cakelet.

Finishing touches

Collar: Roll out a piece of the white fondant until it's $\frac{1}{8}$ in (3 mm) thick and about $5\frac{1}{2}$ in (13.75 cm) long. Cut out a strip $\frac{1}{2}$ in (1.25 cm) wide. Lightly brush the back of the strip with water and adhere it to the neck of the shirt. Using a scriber tool, add lines on the collar for texture.

Stitching: Use a stitching tool to add a stitching effect where the sleeve meets the shirt and along the bottom of the shirt.

Birds: If using the birds and branches motif, roll out the blue fondant until it's $\frac{1}{8}$ in (3 mm) thick. Cut out two birds with the bird cutter. **Ⓑ**

Branches: Using your hands, roll a small amount of the chocolate or brown fondant (or Tootsie Rolls) into a log. Make several cuts on a 45-degree angle into the log, making sure not to cut the log in two. Use your hands to shape the cuts so they look like small branches coming off the main branch. **Ⓒ**

Adhere: Lightly brush the back of the branch with water and adhere to the shirt, starting at one side. Repeat for the other branch and adhere to the other side of the shirt. Lightly brush the back of the birds with water and adhere to the shirt as if they are perching on the branches. Complete the remaining cakelets, if desired.

Additional T-shirt design ideas

- Customize the shirt with someone's name
- Add stripes or polka dots
- Using cake decorating tip #1, write a funny saying or message
- Use various shaped cutters to create limitless T-shirt design variety

Flip-Flop Cakelet

Pool parties, luaus, backyard barbecues—nothing says summer like a pair of flirty flip-flops. To celebrate the sun-worshippers in your life, tint the fondant in their favorite colors, or swap out the medallion for petal-packed flower.

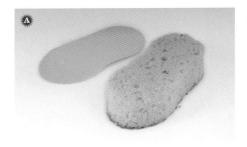

Tools

The Necessities (pages 11–12)
9 x 13-in (23 x 33-cm) cake pan
Flip-Flop template (see Templates, page 115)
Letter presses
$\frac{3}{4}$-in (1.8-cm) circle cutter
1-in (2.5-cm) scallop-edged circle cutter
** (see Resources, page 114)**
Fluted-edged pastry wheel
Flower veiner tool
Stitching tool

Ingredients

One 16-oz (455-g) box cake mix (any flavor)
** prepared, or batter for one 9-in (23-cm)**
** cake**
1 recipe Vanilla Frosting (page 17) or 1
** container store-bought frosting**
8 oz (225 g) white fondant (see Resources,
** page 114)**
$2\frac{1}{2}$ oz (70 g) black fondant (see Resources,
** page 114)**
Pink gel food coloring

Bake the cake

1 Preheat oven to 350°F (180°C). Spray the pan with non-stick spray.

2 Pour the batter into the pan, filling it three-quarters full. Smooth the top and bake for 30 to 40 minutes, or until the top springs back when lightly pressed and a toothpick inserted into the center comes out clean.

3 Place pan on a wire rack to cool for about 10 minutes. If the cake rose above the pan, use a serrated knife to cut away the top of the cake to make it level (set the knife across the top of the pan so you can use it as a guide). Run a knife around the edge to loosen the sides. Invert the cake out of the pan onto a wire rack and allow it to finish cooling. When completely cool, wrap in plastic wrap and freeze for at least two hours until cold and firm.

Prepare to decorate

1 Use the pink gel food coloring to lightly tint a heaping handful (about 6 oz/170 g) of the white fondant (see tinting instructions on page 16). Use the same gel color to tint about 2 oz (55 g) of the white fondant a darker shade of pink. Wrap both separately in plastic wrap until ready to use.

2 Remove cake from the freezer and unwrap. Place the Flip-Flop template on top of the cake and use a sharp knife to cut out the cake around it. ⚫ Remove template and use the knife to clean up any rough edges.

3 Place the cakelet on a piece of parchment. Using a tapered angled spatula, crumb coat the cakelets with Vanilla Frosting starting around the sides of the cake and finishing on the top. Use enough frosting so that the spatula doesn't come into direct contact with the cake. This will keep you from dislodging too many crumbs. (If you find that the cake has thawed and is difficult to coat, rewrap and place in the refrigerator or freezer until firm again.)

Level ***Easy/Intermediate***
Batter yields enough cake for ***4 cakelets***
Fondant quantity listed is suitable to complete ***1 cakelet***

Covering the Cakelet

1 Dust a clean, dry work surface with cornstarch. Roll out the light pink fondant into a sheet $\frac{1}{4}$ in (6 mm) thick and large enough to cover the cakelet.

2 Slide your hands underneath the fondant using open palms so as not to poke a hole in it. Pick the fondant up and gently lay it over the cakelet. Smooth the top first, using an open palm. Then smooth the fondant down over the sides.

3 Use a pastry wheel to cut away excess fondant around the bottom of the cakelet.

Assemble

Sole border

1 Roll out a strip of black fondant until it's $\frac{1}{8}$ in (3 mm) thick and approximately 12 in (30.5 cm) long. Cut out a strip that's 1 in (2.5 cm) wide.

2 Roll out a piece of the dark pink fondant until it's $\frac{1}{8}$ in (3 mm) thick and approximately 12 in (30.5 cm) long. Using a fluted pastry wheel for a scalloped effect, cut out a strip that's $\frac{3}{4}$ in (2 cm) wide.

3 Lightly brush the black strip with water and adhere the dark pink strip to it.

4 Lightly brush water around the bottom of the cakelet and adhere the strip around the bottom of the flip-flop, making sure the seam is in back.

Straps

1 Roll out a piece of black fondant until it's $\frac{1}{8}$ in (3 mm) thick and about $4\frac{1}{2}$ in (11.25 cm) long. Cut out two strips that are 1 in (2.5 cm) wide.

2 Roll out a piece of the dark pink fondant until it's $\frac{1}{8}$ in (3 mm) thick and about $4\frac{1}{2}$ in (11.25 cm) long. Using a fluted pastry wheel for a scalloped effect, cut out two strips that are $\frac{3}{4}$ in (2 cm) wide. ✦

3 Lightly brush the black straps with water and adhere the dark pink strips to them.

4 Use a ball tool to mark the top of the flip-flop where the straps will meet. Apply a dab of water to the marked area and adhere the strap to the sandal. Crumple up a piece of cling wrap and place it under the strap (this will give the strap height while it dries). Add a dab of water to the side of the sandal to adhere the other end of the strap. Use an X-Acto knife to cut away any excess (the strap should meet the top of the pink part of the sole). Repeat this step for the other strap.

Finishing touches

1 Roll out a gumball-sized piece of black fondant until $\frac{1}{8}$ in (3 mm) thick and use the scalloped circle cutter to cut out a fluted circle.

2 Roll out a gumball-sized piece of pink fondant until it's $\frac{1}{8}$ in (3 mm) thick and use a letter press to imprint the letter for the monogram. Next, use the plain circle cutter to cut the monogram out into a circle. ✦ Use a dab of water to adhere the pink monogrammed circle to the black scalloped circle.

3 Use a dab of water to adhere the medallion to the sandal where the straps intersect at the top.

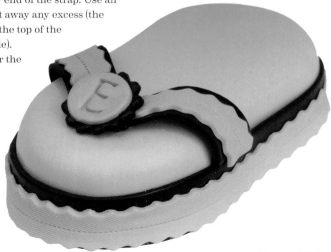

Makeup Kit

When I was young, I used to love sleepovers at my Nana's house. She always planned fun outings, which usually included a trip to the mall. But before we'd leave, she'd inevitably say, "I have to put my face on, then off we'll go!" That was code for, "I never leave the house without my make-up." It always made me smile, and I couldn't wait until I was old enough to put my face on, too.

Tools
The Necessities (pages 11–12)
9 x 13-in (23 x 33-cm) cake pan
¾-in (1.8-cm) circle cutter

Ingredients
One 16-oz (455-g) box cake mix (any flavor)
prepared, or batter for one 9-in (23-cm) cake
1 recipe Vanilla Frosting (page 17) or 1
container store-bought frosting
4 oz (115 g) white fondant (see Resources,
page 114)
8 oz (225 g) black fondant (see Resources,
page 114)
Antique silk luster dust (see Resources,
page 114)
Pink gel food coloring
Ivory gel food coloring

Bake the cake
1 Preheat oven to 350°F (180°C). Spray the pan with non-stick spray.

2 Pour the batter into the pan, filling it three-quarters full. Smooth the top and bake for 30 to 40 minutes, or until the top springs back when lightly pressed and a toothpick inserted into the center comes out clean.

3 Place pan on a wire rack to cool for about 10 minutes. If the cake rose above the pan, use a serrated knife to cut away the top of the cake to make it level (set the knife across the top of the pan so you can use it

as a guide). Run a knife around the edge to loosen the sides, invert the cake out of the pan onto a wire rack and allow to finish cooling. When completely cool, wrap in plastic wrap and freeze for at least two hours until cold and firm.

Prepare to decorate
1 Divide the white fondant into four portions—three of equal size and one slightly larger than the three. Use the pink gel food coloring to tint one portion light pink. Tint another a few shades darker. Tint the largest portion a few shades darker than that. Tint the fourth portion ivory. (See tinting instructions on page 16.) Wrap the four portions separately in plastic wrap until ready to use.

2 Remove cake from the freezer and unwrap. Cut the cake into four equal rectangles. 🔺

Level *Easy*
Batter yields enough cake for *4 cakelets*
Fondant quantity listed is suitable to complete *1 cakelet*

3 Place one rectangle of cake on a piece of parchment. Using a tapered angled spatula, crumb coat the cakelet with Vanilla Frosting starting around the sides of the cake and finishing on the top. Use enough frosting so that the spatula doesn't come into direct contact with the cake. This will keep you from dislodging too many crumbs. (If you find that the cake has thawed and is difficult to coat, re-wrap and place in the refrigerator or freezer until firm again.)

Cover the cakelet

1 Dust a clean, dry work surface with cornstarch. Roll out 6 oz (170 g) of the black fondant into a sheet $\frac{1}{4}$ in (6 mm) thick and large enough to cover the cakelet.

2 Slide your hands underneath the fondant using open palms so as not to poke a hole in it. Pick the fondant up and gently lay it over the cakelet. Smooth the top first, using an open palm. Then smooth the fondant down over the sides.

3 Use a pastry wheel to cut away excess fondant around the bottom of the cakelet.

Assemble

Border: Roll out a strip of black fondant until it's $\frac{1}{8}$ in (3 mm) thick and approximately 14 in (35.5 cm) long. Cut out a strip that's 1 in (2.5 cm) wide. Lightly brush the base of the cakelet with water and adhere the strip with the seam placed in the back.

Eye shadow: Roll out the tinted fondants

until $\frac{1}{8}$ in (3 mm) thick. Use a circle cutter to cut out one circle from each for a total of 4 circles. Dust the pink and ivory circles with antique silk luster dust and adhere to the cakelet with a dab of water. ☀ For a more realistic effect, use the circle cutter and an X-Acto knife to excise recesses in the black fondant so that the makeup can be set into the surface of the kit.

Blush: Using one of the darker shades of rolled-out pink fondant, cut out a 2 x 1-in (5 x 2.5-cm) rectangle to make the blush. Adhere

to the left side of the makeup kit with a dab of water, or set it into the corresponding recess if you've opted to use cut-outs.

Eye shadow brushes: Roll out a small portion of black fondant until $\frac{1}{4}$ in (6 mm) thick. Cut two strips approximately 2 in (5 cm) long and $\frac{1}{4}$ in (6 mm) wide. Roll a small bit of black fondant into two small balls, slightly flatten with your finger, and adhere the black strips to make the tip of the eye shadow brushes. Adhere brushes to the near edge of the makeup kit with water.

Tiers of Joy

Level *Intermediate*
Batter yields enough cake for *2 cakelets*
Fondant quantity listed is suitable to complete *1 cakelet*

This two-tiered cake may be small, but it makes a big impression—especially when presented as the basis for of a collection of individually decorated cakes. It truly is a blank canvas, and I love all the possibilities it offers. Because it's cut from a sheet cake, you can use cutters in different sizes and shapes to create a wide array of cakes. When adorning your cake, consider adding things like a monogram, ruffles, geometric shapes, flowers, and vines or stripes. Look through wedding magazines for ideas, or just let your imagination fly.

Tools

The Necessities (pages 11–12)
9 x 13-in (23 x 33-cm) cake pan
Medium petal cutter
Flower veiner tool
2 fondant smoothers
1 medium blossom cutter
1 small blossom cutter

Ingredients

One 16-oz (455-g) box cake mix (any flavor)
  prepared, or batter for one 9-in (23-cm) cake
1 recipe Vanilla Frosting (page 17) or 1
  container store-bought frosting
1 lb (455 g) white fondant
  (see Resources, page 114)
4 oz (115 g) red fondant
  (see Resources, page 114)
Blue gel food coloring

Bake the cake

1 Preheat oven to 350°F (180°C). Prepare the cake batter. Spray the pan with non-stick spray.

2 Pour the batter into the pan, filling it three-quarters full. Smooth the top and bake for 30 to 45 minutes, or until the top springs back when lightly pressed and a toothpick inserted into the center comes out clean.

3 Place pan on a wire rack to cool for about 10 minutes. If the cake rose above the pan, use a serrated knife to cut away the top of the cake to make it level (set the knife across the top of the pan so you can use it as a guide). Run a knife around the edge to loosen the sides. Invert the cake out of the pan onto a wire rack and allow it to finish cooling. When completely cool, wrap in plastic wrap and freeze for at least two hours until cold and firm.

Prepare to decorate

1 Reserve a gumball-sized portion of white fondant for use in the center of the flower. Use the blue gel food coloring to tint the remainder of the white fondant. (See tinting instructions on page 16.) Wrap tightly with plastic wrap until ready to use.

2 Remove the cake from the freezer and unwrap from the plastic wrap. Cut out two 4-in (10-cm) squares for the bottom tier and two 2½-in (6.25-cm) squares for the top tier.

3 Spread a layer of Vanilla Frosting between the two cake layers of each tier.

4 Place a tier on a piece of parchment. Using a tapered angled spatula, crumb coat with

Vanilla Frosting starting around the sides of the cake and finishing on the top. Use enough frosting so that the spatula doesn't come into direct contact with the cake. This will keep you from dislodging too many crumbs. (If you find that the cake has thawed and is difficult to coat, re-wrap and place in the refrigerator or freezer until firm again.) Repeat with the remaining tier.

Covering the cakelet

1 Dust your work surface with cornstarch. Roll out a piece of blue fondant $\frac{1}{4}$ in (6 mm) thick and approximately 10 in (25.5 cm) square.

2 Slide your hand under the fondant and gently place it onto the 4-in (10-cm) square tier. Using an open palm or a fondant smoother, smooth the top. Using two fondant smoothers, gently press and smooth the opposite sides of the cake at the same time. Repeat with the other sides. Cut away excess fondant using a pastry wheel.

3 To cover the $2\frac{1}{2}$-in (6.25-cm) square tier, roll out a piece of fondant $\frac{1}{4}$ in (6 mm) thick and approximately 6 in (15 cm) square. Repeat the instructions in step 2 above to cover and smooth the tier.

Assemble

1 Roll out a piece of blue fondant $\frac{1}{2}$ in (1.25 cm) wide and approximately 16 in (40.5 cm) long.

2 Roll out a piece of red fondant $\frac{1}{4}$ in (6 mm) wide and approximately 16 in (40.5 cm) long.

3 Lightly brush water along the blue strip and lay the red strip on top, aligning the bottom edge.

4 Lightly brush water along the bottom of the bottom tier of the cakelet and attach the blue fondant strip with the seams in the back. Cut away any excess fondant with scissors.

5 Spread a small circle of Vanilla Frosting atop the center of the bottom tier. Place the smaller tier on top.

6 Roll out a piece of blue fondant $\frac{1}{2}$ in (1.25 cm) wide and approximately 10 in (25.5 cm) long.

7 Roll out a piece of red fondant $\frac{1}{4}$ in (6 mm) wide and approximately 10 in (25.5 cm) long.

8 Lightly brush water along the blue strip and lay the red strip on top, aligning the bottom edge.

9 Lightly brush water along the bottom border of the top tier and attach the blue fondant strip to the cake, aligning the seams in the back. Cut away any excess fondant with scissors.

10 Use a small ball tool to add linear texture to the red bands.

Finishing touches

1 Dust your work surface with cornstarch. Roll out a piece of the red fondant $\frac{1}{8}$ in (3 mm) thick. Use the petal cutter to cut out six petals.

2 Using a small ball tool, thin out the edges of the petals and add linear texture to the flower. ☀

3 Use water and a small paintbrush to adhere the petals in the shape of a flower to the border of the top tier.

4 Roll out a small ball of red fondant and cut out one blossom using the medium blossom cutter. Adhere the red blossom to the center of the flower petals with a dab of water.

5 Roll out a small ball of white fondant and cut out one blossom using the small blossom cutter. Adhere the white blossom to center of the red blossom with a dab of water.

6 Roll a small ball of white fondant and adhere to the center of the flower. You may use a toothpick to poke several holes into the flower's center to add a stippled texture.

Chapter 4

Good Enough to Eat

Cup o' Joe

Level **Easy**
Batter yields enough cake for **4 cakelets**
Fondant quantity listed is suitable to complete **1 cakelet**

This design is great for coffee junkies and tea lovers, of course, but it's also the perfect symbol of friendship. After all, when we've got news to share, need a shoulder to cry on, or just want to catch up, we get together with friends over coffee, right? You can follow these instructions to make a sweet and girly cup, or customize it to suit the taste of your particular friend.

Tools
6-cavity Wilton king-size muffin pan
The Necessities (pages 11–12)
Medium daisy flower cutter
4-in (10-cm) circle cutter
Coffee Cup Handle template
  (see Templates, page 115)
Flower Pot template
  (see Templates, page 115)
Toothpick

Ingredients
One 16-oz (455-g) box cake mix (any flavor)
  prepared, or batter for one 9-in (23-cm) cake
1 recipe Vanilla Frosting (page 17) or 1
  container store-bought frosting
1 recipe Royal Icing (page 17)
12 oz (340 g) white fondant
  (see Resources, page 114)
1 oz (30 g) chocolate or brown fondant
Pink gel food coloring
Green gel food coloring
1 tablespoon vodka

Create the cup handle (2–3 days prior to decorating)
1 Color 8 oz (225 g) of the white fondant with the pink gel food coloring. (See tinting instructions on page 16.) Pinch off about 2 oz (55 g) to make the handle. Wrap the rest in plastic wrap until ready to use.

2 Dust a clean, dry work surface with cornstarch. Roll the fondant out into a log 4 in (10 cm) long and ¼ in (6 mm) thick. Use the handle template as a guide to shape the log into a handle.

3 Place the handle on a piece of parchment paper and set aside to dry out for at least two days at room temperature out of direct sunlight (to keep the color from fading).

Bake the cake
1 Preheat oven to 350°F (180°C). Spray each of the king-size muffin pan cavities to be used with non-stick spray (you will need one muffin cake for one cakelet). Fill each cavity being used three-quarters full with batter. Bake for 25 minutes, or until the top springs back when lightly pressed and a toothpick inserted into the center comes out clean.

2 Allow the cake to cool for a few minutes in the pan. If the cake rose above the pan, use a serrated knife to cut away the top to make it level (set the knife across the top of the pan so you can use it as a guide). Run a knife around the edge to loosen the sides. Invert the cake out of the pan and place on a wire rack to finish cooling. When completely cool, wrap the cake in plastic wrap and freeze for at least two hours until cold and firm.

Prepare to decorate
1 Remove the cake from the freezer and unwrap. ✴ Place it upside down on a square piece of parchment paper. Using a tapered angled spatula, apply a smooth crumb coat of Vanilla Frosting on the cake, but do not ice the top. Use enough frosting so that the spatula doesn't come into direct contact with the cake. This will keep you from dislodging too many crumbs.

2 Dust the work surface with cornstarch. Roll out the remaining pink fondant into a 4 ½-in (11.25-cm) by 11-in (28-cm) rectangle that's ¼ in (6 mm) thick. Place the Flower Pot template on top and use a pastry wheel or X-Acto knife to cut out the shape, using the template as a guide.

3 Gently pick up the fondant and wrap it around the cake so that the seams touch. Cut away any excess fondant around the bottom of the cake.

4 Place a parchment square on top of the cakelet and turn it right side up. Refrigerate for one hour.

Assemble
Coffee: Crumb coat the top of the coffee cup with Vanilla Frosting. Roll out the chocolate fondant until it's $\frac{1}{8}$ in (3 mm) thick. Use a 4-in (10-cm) circle cutter to cut out a circle and place on top of the coffee cup.

Rim
1 Roll out a strip of white fondant $\frac{3}{4}$ in (1.8 cm) wide and about 12 in (30.5 cm) long. Straighten the edges with a pastry wheel.

2 Color 2 oz (55 g) of white fondant with the green gel food coloring. (See tinting instructions on page 16.)

3 Roll out 1 oz (30 g) of green fondant into a strip about $\frac{1}{4}$ in (6 mm) wide and approximately 12 in (30.5 cm) long.

4 Use a little water to adhere the green strip to the middle of the white strip.

5 Lightly brush water around the lip of the cup. Match the end of the white and green strip to the seam of the cup. The strip should rise slightly higher than the top of the cup.

6 Wrap the strip around the cup. Cut away any excess and seal the seam with a dab of water.

Handle: Place a dab of royal icing at the top and bottom curves of the handle. Gently press the handle in place at the fondant seam. Hold in place for at least 30 seconds until the handle is securely attached. (Be careful not touch the handle while you continue to decorate the cup.)

Finishing touches
Decorative scroll: Roll out a piece of green fondant approximately 5 in (12.7 cm) long and $\frac{1}{4}$ in (6 mm) thick, with tapered ends. Brush water onto the cup in the shape that you want the scroll to be. Then press the green fondant roll along your painted outline. The green fondant scroll should be in the shape suitable for the central placement of your flower.

Daisy: Roll out a piece of the remaining pink fondant and use a medium-size daisy flower cutter to cut out the flower. Dab the center of the green decorative scroll with water and attach the flower by gently pressing it into place.

Center of daisy: Roll a small ball of white fondant and adhere it to the center of the flower with water. Use a toothpick to poke multiple holes in the white ball for a stippled texture.

Cream scroll: Brush the entire brown circle (the "coffee") with vodka to give it a realistic sheen. Roll a small piece of white fondant into a small thin log and adhere it to the coffee in a spiral design.

Sushi Bar

I love playing with people's expectations by making sweet cakelets that look like savory foods we know and love. Sushi is a perfect example. White sprinkles stand in for rice and orange nonpareils for the tiny orange flying fish roe, or tobiko. And you can mold the fondant into any number of traditional sushi combos.

Tools
9 x 6-in (23 x 15-cm) metal brownie pan
The Necessities (pages 11–12)
Linen texture sheet

Ingredients
One 16-oz (455-g) box cake mix (any flavor) prepared, or batter for one 9-in (23-cm) cake
1 recipe Vanilla Frosting (page 17) or 1 container store-bought icing
4 oz (225 g) green fondant (see Resources, page 114)
3 oz (280 g) golden yellow fondant (see Resources, page 114)
6 oz (115 g) white fondant (see Resources, page 114)
Orange nonpareils
White sprinkles or white nonpareils
Copper gel food coloring

Bake the cake
1 Preheat oven to 350°F (180°C). Prepare the cake batter. Spray the brownie pan with non-stick spray.

2 Pour the batter into the pan, filling it three-quarters full. Smooth the top and bake for 20 to 30 minutes, or until the top springs back when lightly pressed and a toothpick inserted into the center comes out clean.

3 Place pan on a wire rack to cool for about 10 minutes. If the cake rose above the pan, use a serrated knife to cut away the top of the cake to make it level (set the knife across the top of the pan so you can use it as a guide). Run a knife around the edge to loosen the sides. Invert the cake out of the pan onto a wire rack and allow to finish cooling. When completely cool, wrap in plastic wrap and freeze for at least two hours until cold and firm.

Make the sushi
Whitefish
1 Dust a clean, dry surface with cornstarch. Roll out 3 oz (85 g) of white fondant into a strip $\frac{1}{4}$ in (6 mm) thick, 1 in (2.5 cm) wide and $3\frac{1}{2}$ in (8.75 cm) long.

2 Lightly roll one end of the strip to make it slightly thinner in width. Use your fingers to round the corners.

3 Use the fondant marking tool to score rows of arcs along the entire strip.

Egg
1 Dust a clean, dry surface with cornstarch. Roll out 3 oz (85 g) of golden yellow fondant and cut into a rectangular strip approximately $3\frac{1}{2}$ in (8.75 cm) by $1\frac{1}{2}$ in (3.75 cm).

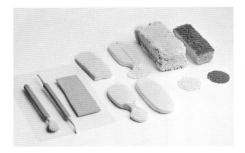

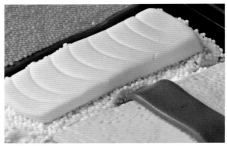

2 Press the linen impression sheet into the top of the fondant for a textured effect. You can also lay a piece of cling wrap over the fondant and gently press the coarse side of a sponge onto the fondant to make the impression.

Shrimp
1 Dust a clean, dry surface with cornstarch. Roll out 3 oz (85 g) of white fondant into a strip $\frac{1}{4}$ in (6 mm) thick, 1 in (2.5 cm) wide and $3\frac{1}{2}$ in (8.75 cm) long.

2 Use your fingers to pinch the strip halfway between the middle and one end to create the tail. Use the fondant marking tool to repeatedly score lines across the tail.

Level *Easy/Intermediate*
Batter yields enough cake for **1 set of 4 sushi mini-cakelets**
Fondant quantity listed is suitable to complete **1 set of 4 sushi mini-cakelets**

3 Above the tail, score a vertical line down the middle of the shrimp. With the same tool, score arcs on both sides of the middle line.

4 On a small plate, combine four drops of copper gel food coloring and one drop of water to dilute the gel. Dip the paintbrush in a cup of water then dab it in the copper gel/water mixture.

5 Start coloring the shrimp by painting the tail, making sure to get the food coloring in the lines covering the entire tail. The more gel food coloring you put on your brush, the darker the color on the shrimp.

6 Dip the brush in the cup of water to dilute the color on the brush, then paint over the entire body of the shrimp. This will make the white fondant take on a light coral color.

7 Finally, dip the brush in the gel food coloring mixture and brush inside the lines you created with the marking tool. This will bring out the details in the shrimp.

8 Dip the brush into the cup of water one last time and brush over the entire shrimp.

Prepare to decorate

1 Remove cake from the freezer and unwrap. Place on a piece of parchment bottom side up.

2 Cut the cake into four strips $4\frac{1}{2}$ in (11.25 cm) long and 2 in (5 cm) wide.

3 Using a tapered angled spatula, crumb coat the cakelets with Vanilla Frosting starting at the sides and finishing at the top. Use enough frosting so that the spatula doesn't come into direct contact with the cake. This will keep you from dislodging too many crumbs.

4 Pour the white sprinkles or nonpareils in a shallow bowl or plate. Roll three of the cakelets in the sprinkles.

Assemble

1 Dust a clean, dry surface with cornstarch. Roll out 3 oz (85 g) of green fondant into a strip $\frac{1}{8}$ in (3 mm) thick, 2 in (5 cm) wide and 10 in (25.5 cm) long.

2 Wrap the fondant strip around the cakelet that's not coated in sprinkles. Sprinkle a generous layer of orange nonpareils on top.

3 Place the fondant whitefish, shrimp, and egg on top of the remaining cakelets that are covered in white sprinkles or nonpareils, securing them to the cakes with a dab of icing.

4 Dust a clean, dry surface with cornstarch. Roll out 1 oz (30 g) of green fondant into a strip $\frac{1}{8}$ in (3 mm) thick, 1 in (2.5 cm) wide and 5 in (12.5 cm) long. Wrap the strip across the egg cakelet. Secure the strip in place with a dab of icing.

An Apple a Day

Before I launched Cupcake Envy I was a public school music teacher, and in the seven years I taught, I never received an apple. Instead my kids treated me to dozens of delicious homemade cookies, fudge and brownies. This cheerful cakelet takes the old "teacher's apple" cliché and turns it into something teachers really crave—sweets!

Tools

6-cavity mini ball pan
The Necessities (pages 11–12)
Double-sided leaf veiner
Medium-size leaf cutter

Ingredients

One 16-oz (455-g) box cake mix (any flavor)
  prepared, or batter for one 9-in (23-cm) cake
1 recipe Vanilla Frosting (page 17) or 1
  container store-bought frosting
6 oz (170 g) red fondant
  (see Resources, page 114)
2 oz (55 g) chocolate fondant
  (see Resources, page 114)
1 oz (28 g) green fondant
  (see Resources, page 114)
One 2-in segment uncooked spaghetti

Bake the cakes

1 Preheat oven to 350°F (180°C). Spray each of the mini ball cavities to be used with non-stick spray (you will need two mini ball cakes for one cakelet). Fill each cavity being used three-quarters full with batter. Bake for 10 to 12 minutes, or until the tops spring back when lightly pressed and a toothpick inserted into the center comes out clean.

2 Allow the cakes to cool for a few minutes in the pan. If the cakes rose above the pan, use a serrated knife to trim the cakes until they are level (use the top of the pan as your guide). Run a knife around the edge to loosen the sides. Invert the cakes out of the pan onto a wire rack to finish cooling. When completely cool, wrap each in plastic wrap and freeze for at least two hours until cold and firm.

Make the stem

1 While the cakes chill, roll chocolate fondant into a rope $\frac{1}{4}$ in (6 mm) thick and 2 in (5 cm) long.

2 Use your thumb to gently flatten one end of the stem.

3 Insert a piece of raw spaghetti into the base of the stem.

4 Place the stem on a piece of parchment paper and set aside.

Prepare the cakelet

1 Place each cake flat side down on a piece of parchment and cut away any hard edges.

2 Using a tapered angled spatula, apply a layer of Vanilla Frosting to the flat bottom of one of the ball cakes. Adhere the flat bottom of another cake to the frosted surface to form a sphere.

3 Cut away any rough edges where the two halves meet to make for a smooth seam. At the top of the apple, cut a cone-shaped piece of cake out of the sphere using a serrated knife.

4 Crumb coat the sphere with Vanilla Frosting. Use enough frosting so that the

Level *Easy*
Batter yields enough cake for *3 cakelets*
Fondant quantity listed is suitable to complete *1 cakelet*

spatula doesn't come into direct contact with the cake. This will keep you from dislodging too many crumbs.

Cover the cakelet

1 Dust a clean, dry work surface with cornstarch. Roll out the red fondant into a circle $\frac{1}{4}$ in (6 mm) thick and no larger than a dinner plate.

2 Place fondant on top of a cakelet (with the incised cone facing up) and smooth it down and around the cake.

3 Cut away excess fondant with a pastry wheel.

4 Use your fingers to gently press into the top of the apple in a circular motion. This will give the apple its proper shape and will create a space where you can insert the stem.

5 Place the fondant-covered cakelet in the refrigerator to chill for 30 minutes.

Decorate

1 Dust a clean, dry work surface with cornstarch. Roll out a small amount of green fondant until it's $\frac{1}{8}$ in (3 mm) thick.

2 Cut out one leaf using a medium-size leaf cutter.

3 Lightly dust both the top and bottom of the double-sided leaf veiner with cornstarch and place the green fondant leaf form onto the bottom veiner. Place the top of the veiner on top of the fondant leaf and gently squeeze

the veiner together so that the fondant leaf will have a texture on both sides.

4 Dab a little water in the indentation at the top of the apple. Adhere the leaf, bending

and draping it over the side of the apple to give it a natural curve.

5 Gently insert the chocolate fondant stem into the top of the apple to secure it.

Not-So-Baby Cake(let)

Larger-than-life friends with big personalities deserve a cupcake that makes a real statement. When you need a personal-size treat that speaks volumes, this is the cakelet to make.

Tools

6-cavity Wilton king-size muffin pan
4-cavity Wilton mini ball cake pan
The Necessities (pages 11–12)
Flower Pot template (see Templates, page 115)

Ingredients

One 16-oz (455-g) box cake mix (any flavor)
   prepared, or batter for one 9-in (23-cm) cake
1 recipe Vanilla Frosting (page 17) or 1
   container store-bought icing
6 oz (170 g) black fondant
   (see Resources, page 114)
4 oz (115 g) white fondant
   (see Resources, page 114)
2 oz (55 g) red fondant
1 oz (28 g) chocolate or brown fondant
Pink gel food coloring
One 2-in (5-cm) segment of uncooked spaghetti
1 tablespoon vodka

Bake the cakes

1 Preheat oven to 350°F (180°C). Spray each muffin-pan and mini-ball-pan cavity to be used with non-stick spray (you will need one muffin cake and one mini ball cake for one cakelet). Fill each cavity being used three-quarters full with batter. Bake the muffin pan for 25 minutes and the ball pan for 10–12 minutes, or until the tops spring back when lightly pressed and a toothpick inserted into the center comes out clean.

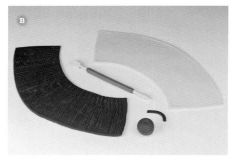

2 Allow the cakes to cool completely in the pans. If the cakes rose above the pan, use a serrated knife to cut away the tops to make them level (set the knife across the top of the pan so you can use it as a guide). Run a knife around the edge to loosen the sides. Invert the cakes out of the pan. ☀ Wrap each in plastic and freeze for at least two hours until cold and firm.

Prepare the top

1 Remove the mini ball cake from the freezer and unwrap.

2 Place the mini ball cake on a piece of parchment. Using a tapered angled spatula, crumb coat the cake with Vanilla Frosting. Use enough frosting so that the spatula doesn't come into direct contact with the cake. This will keep you from dislodging too many crumbs.

3 Use pink gel food coloring to tint the white fondant (see tinting instructions on page 16).

4 Dust a clean, dry work surface with cornstarch. Roll out the pink fondant into a sheet $\frac{1}{4}$ in (6 mm) thick.

5 Lay the pink fondant on top of the mini ball "dome." Use your hands to smooth the fondant over the top. Cut away excess fondant with a pastry wheel.

6 Starting at the top, use a large ball tool or your fingers to press a line spiraling down around the entire dome. This will give a swirled look to your "frosting." Place the finished dome in the fridge to chill.

Prepare the bottom

1 Remove the king-size muffin cake from the freezer and unwrap. Place upside down (wide-end down) on a piece of parchment. This will be the base of the cupcake.

2 Using a tapered angled spatula, crumb coat the sides of the cakelet (but not the top) with Vanilla Frosting. Use enough frosting so that the spatula doesn't come into direct contact

Level *Easy/Intermediate*
Batter yields enough cake for *2 cakelets*
Fondant quantity listed is suitable to complete *1 cakelet*

with the cake. This will keep you from dislodging too many crumbs.

3 Dust a clean, dry work surface with cornstarch. Roll out the black fondant into a sheet $\frac{1}{4}$ in (6 mm) thick.

4 Place the Flower Pot template on top of the fondant and cut out the shape using a pastry wheel or an X-Acto knife.

5 Use the fondant marking tool to score vertical lines over the entire surface of the sheet of black fondant. ✹

6 Wrap the black fondant neatly around the bottom cake. Cut away excess fondant with a pastry wheel.

7 Place a parchment square on top of the cakelet and turn it right side up (wide end on top).

Assemble

1 Coat the top of the base "wrapper" cake with Vanilla Frosting.

2 Remove the pink cake top from the refrigerator and gently place it atop the base cake.

3 Smooth the top of the black fondant wrapper up to meet the pink cupcake top so that no cake remains exposed.

4 Lightly brush the entire black cupcake wrapper with vodka to give it shine.

The cherry on top

1 Roll out a thin log of chocolate or brown fondant approximately $2\frac{1}{2}$ in (6.5 cm) long.

2 Insert the piece of raw spaghetti into one end of the brown fondant stem.

3 Form a slight arc in the end of the brown fondant stem and place it on a piece of parchment paper.

4 Roll the red fondant into a large gumball shape.

5 Use the cone tip of your fondant tool to create an indentation in the cherry and then insert the stem into it.

6 Adhere the cherry to the top of the cupcake with a dab of water.

High Tea

A cup of tea can mean so many things, from a symbol of friendship to one of sympathy. Whatever the occasion, this teacup always works beautifully.

Tools

The Necessities (pages 11–12)
9 x 6-in (23 x 15-cm) metal brownie pan
6-cavity Wilton mini wonder mold baking pan
Teacup Handle template (see Templates, page 115)
2 circle cutters: 4 in (10 cm) and $\frac{3}{4}$ in (1.8 cm) diameter
Piping bag
Cake decorating tip #4

Ingredients

One 16-oz (455-g) box cake mix (any flavor) prepared, or batter for one 9-in (23-cm) cake
1 recipe Vanilla Frosting (page 17) or 1 container store-bought frosting
1 lb (445 g) white fondant (see Resources, page 114)
2 oz (55 g) chocolate or brown fondant (see Resources, page 114)
$\frac{1}{2}$ cup (115 g) Royal Icing (page 17)
Yellow gel food coloring
Pink gel food coloring
Green gel food coloring
Blue gel food coloring

Create the cup handle (2–3 days prior to decorating)

1 Tint 8 oz (225 g) of the white fondant yellow. See tinting instructions on page 16.

2 Roll out a log of yellow fondant approximately $\frac{1}{4}$ in (6 mm) thick and 2 in (5 cm) long. Use the Teacup Handle template

as a guide to shape the log into a handle.

3 Place the handle on parchment to dry for 2–3 days at room temperature out of direct sunlight (to keep color from fading). Wrap extra fondant in plastic wrap until ready to use.

4 Tint 2 oz (55 g) of the white fondant green, 4 oz (115 g) blue and 2 oz (55 g) pink. Wrap each color in plastic wrap until ready to use.

Bake the cakes

1 Preheat oven to 350°F (180°C). Prepare the cake batter. Spray the brownie pan and each mini wonder mold pan cavity to be used with non-stick spray (you will need one mini wonder mold cake for one cakelet).

2 Pour the batter into the prepared pans, filling each three-quarters full. Smooth the top and bake the brownie pan for 20–30 minutes, and the mini wonder mold pan for 12–14 minutes, or until the tops spring back when lightly pressed and a toothpick inserted into the center comes out clean.

3 Place pans on a wire rack

to cool for about 10 minutes. If the cakes rose above the pan, use a serrated knife to cut away the tops of the cakes to make them level (set the knife across the top of each pan so you can use it as a guide). Run a knife around the edge to loosen the sides. Invert the cakes out of the pan onto a wire rack and allow to finish cooling. When completely cool, wrap them in plastic wrap and freeze for at least two hours until cold and firm.

Prepare to decorate

1 Remove the cakes from the freezer and unwrap. Place a mini wonder mold cake upside down on a piece of parchment.

Level *Intermediate*
Batter yields enough cake for *2 cakelets*
Fondant quantity listed is suitable to complete *1 cakelet*

2 Using a tapered angled spatula, crumb coat the cake with Vanilla Frosting, starting at the sides and finishing at the top. Use enough frosting so that the spatula doesn't come into direct contact with the cake. This will keep you from dislodging too many crumbs.

3 Use the 4-in (10-cm) circle cutter to cut a circle out of the brownie pan cake. Place the cake on a piece of parchment. (It will be the saucer.)

4 Use a spoon to scoop out a circle $\frac{1}{4}$ in (6 mm) deep from the center of the cake, where the teacup will be placed.

5 Using a tapered angled spatula, crumb coat the top and sides of the saucer cake. Refriger-ate until firm.

Covering the cakelet

1 Dust a clean, dry work surface with cornstarch. Roll out the yellow fondant into a sheet $\frac{1}{4}$ in (6 mm) thick. Divide it into two pieces.

2 Wrap a piece of fondant around the mini wonder mold cakelet. Use a pastry wheel to cut away excess fondant around the bottom of the cake. Refrigerate.

3 Lay a piece of fondant over the saucer cakelet, smoothing it over the top and around the sides. Use a pastry wheel to cut away the excess. Refrigerate.

Assemble

1 Remove the cakes from the refrigerator.

2 Apply water to center of the saucer cakelet and adhere the saucer to the teacup.

3 Place a parchment square on top of the cakelet and turn it right side up.

4 Dust a clean, dry work surface with cornstarch and roll out the chocolate or brown fondant until it is $\frac{1}{8}$ in (3 mm) thick.

5 Use the 4-in (10-cm) circle cutter to cut out a circle.

6 Thinly coat the top of the cakelet with Vanilla Frosting and adhere the brown circle.

7 Fill a piping bag fitted with a #4 tip with royal icing. Pipe dots around the top of the teacup, covering the seam where the yellow fondant and brown fondant circle meet.

Finishing touches

1 Dust a clean, dry work surface with cornstarch. Roll out the blue, pink, and green fondants into sheets $\frac{1}{8}$ in (3 mm) thick.

2 Cut out an assortment of circles using the small circle cutter.

3 Adhere the circles randomly to the teacup using a dab of water.

4 Dab the top and bottom of the teacup handle with royal icing. Gently press the

handle against the teacup. Hold in place for at least 30 seconds, until the handle is firmly planted onto the teacup.

5 Dust a clean, dry work surface with cornstarch. Roll out some blue fondant into a strip $\frac{1}{8}$ in (3 mm) thick, 1 in (2.5 cm) wide, and 10 in (25.5 cm) long. Adhere the strip around the bottom of the saucer using water and a paint brush.

At the Market

Level *Intermediate/Difficult*
Batter yields enough cake for *1 cakelet*
Fondant quantity listed is suitable to complete *1 cakelet*

My mother is an amazing cook, and I can still vividly recall how excited I would get when I would see her coming home from the market with bags filled with goodies. Warm baguettes, fresh vegetables and at least two meats (yes two!) graced our dinner table every night. Mom showered us in culinary love, and it all started with those brown paper grocery bags. This one's for you, Mom.

Tools
9 x 6-in (23 x 15-cm) metal brownie pan
The Necessities (pages 11–12)
¾-in (18-mm) circle cutter
Fondant smoother
Toothpick

Ingredients
One 16-oz (455 g) box cake mix (any flavor) prepared, or batter for one 9-in (23-cm) cake
1 recipe Vanilla Frosting (page 17) or 1 container store-bought frosting
1 lb (455 g) white fondant (see Resources, page 114)
2 oz (55 g) chocolate or brown fondant (see Resources, page 114)
6 oz (170 g) red fondant
Gel food colorings: leaf green, pink, ivory, orange, and purple

Create the groceries (2–3 days prior to decorating)
After shaping the fondant groceries, place on a piece of parchment paper and set aside to dry out for at least two days at room temperature out of direct sunlight (to keep the colors from fading).

Carrots
1 Tint 3 oz (85 g) of white fondant with the orange gel food coloring. Divide the fondant into three equal pieces and roll each into a small log. Use the fondant smoother to apply pressure to one end of the fondant logs to create a narrowed end. Use the scoring tool to impress horizontal lines across each log. Use a small ball tool to create an indent on the top of each carrot.

2 Tint 4 oz (115 g) of white fondant with the green gel food coloring. Roll a small portion into a thin sheet and cut it into tiny strips. Gather the strips into three bunches and pinch on one end. With a dab of water, adhere the gathered green strips to the top of each carrot. ⚽

Cabbage
1 Roll a gumball-sized ball of green fondant for the middle of the cabbage. Roll green fondant into a sheet ⅛ in (3 mm) thick. Use the circle cutter to cut out approximately six ¾-in (1.8-cm) circles for the cabbage leaves.

2 Use the ball tool to thin the edges of the circles. Use a little water to adhere the leaves to the green fondant ball. Begin by wrapping the leaves around the middle of the fondant ball so that the leaves cover the top of the cabbage. Then continue wrapping leaves around the lower part of the fondant ball.

Baguettes
Tint 1 oz (28 g) white fondant with the ivory gel color. Reserve a small pinch to make the cork for the wine bottle (see page 56). Divide the remaining fondant in half and roll out

purple gel food coloring. Use the fondant smoother to roll it out into a log $\frac{3}{4}$ in (1.8 cm) thick and $2\frac{1}{2}$ in (6.25 cm) long. Use the fondant smoother to apply pressure to one half of the fondant log to create a narrowed end. Use the small ball tool to indent the top of the bottle.

2 Use the reserved pinch of ivory fondant to create the cork. Roll it into a ball and adhere to the top of the bottle with a little water. Use a toothpick to poke multiple holes in the cork for a stippled look.

Bake the cake

1 Preheat oven to 350°F (180°C). Prepare the cake batter. Spray the brownie pan with non-stick spray.

2 Pour the batter into the pan, filling it three-quarters full. Smooth the top and bake for 20 to 30 minutes, or until the top springs back when lightly pressed and a toothpick inserted into the center comes out clean.

3 Place pan on a wire rack to cool for about 10 minutes. If the cake rose above the pan, use a serrated knife to cut away the top of the cake to make it level (set the knife across the top of the pan so you can use it as a guide). Run a knife around the edge to loosen the sides. Invert the cake out of the pan onto a wire rack and allow to finish cooling. When completely cool, wrap in plastic wrap and freeze for at least two hours until cold and firm.

each into logs approximately $1\frac{1}{2}$ in (3.75 cm) long. Use the fondant smoother to apply pressure to one end to create a narrowed end. Use the scoring tool to score two or three horizontal lines on each log.

Peppers

1 Divide the red fondant into three marble-sized balls. Press the veiner tool into the top of the each ball to make an indentation. Use the scoring tool to create the creases around the sides of the ball.

2 Roll out a pinch of green fondant into three small, thin logs to make the stems. Use a little water to adhere each to the top of a pepper.

Bouquet of flowers

1 Tint 2 oz (55 g) of white fondant with the pink gel food coloring. Roll out into a sheet $\frac{1}{8}$ in (3 mm) thick. Using the small flower cutter, cut out 15–20 flowers.

2 Roll out a small amount of green fondant into a thin sheet. Cut out a 2-in (5-cm) x 1-in (2.5-cm) rectangle, and fringe one long edge with an X-Acto knife. Roll up the strip.

3 Adhere the flowers to the ends of the fringe with a dab of water.

Bottle of Wine

1 Tint 2 oz (55 g) of white fondant using the

Prepare to decorate

1 Knead together 2 oz (55 g) of the chocolate or brown fondant with 4 oz (115 g) of the white fondant to create the grocery bag color. Wrap fondant in plastic wrap until ready to use.

2 Remove the cake from the freezer and unwrap. Use a serrated knife to cut it in half to form two $4\frac{1}{2}$ x 3-in (11.25 x 7.5-cm) rectangles. ☀ Reserve half for another use.

3 Place cake upright on a piece of parchment. Using a tapered angled spatula, crumb coat the sides of the cakelet with Vanilla Frosting (don't coat the top). Use enough frosting so that the spatula doesn't come into direct contact with the cake. This will keep you from dislodging too many crumbs.

Cover the cakelet

1 Dust a clean, dry work surface with cornstarch. Roll out the light brown fondant into a sheet 10 in (25.5 cm) long and 5 in (12.5 cm) wide and $\frac{1}{4}$ in (6 mm) thick.

2 Set the iced cake onto the fondant, allowing for extra fondant where the top of the bag will be. (You want the fondant to be a little higher than the cake to give the impression of a bag and so you can add the groceries coming out of the top.) Use the zig-zag wheel on the pastry cutter to give the edge the effect of the top of a grocery bag. Gently wrap the fondant around the cake. The fondant seam should be in a back corner. Smooth with palms or a fondant smoother.

3 Once the cake is completely wrapped, stand the cake upright onto a piece of parchment.

Assemble

1 To make the bag creases, use the scoring tool to mark a triangle at the bottom of each side of the bag. Starting at the top of the triangle, score a straight line up to the top of the bag.

2 Apply Vanilla Frosting onto the exposed cake at the top of the bag.

3 Set the dried fondant groceries into the frosting. Arrange them so that the bag looks full and you can see the assortment.

Chapter 5

Oh Baby!

You're the Onesie

There are some pretty questionable baby shower cakes out there—cakes shaped like actual babies (ouch!) or diapers (ick!). But a teeny-tiny onesie is just plain cute, and a perfect way to celebrate a mommy-to-be. Pink or blue, sweet or trendy, this cakelet offers a versatile design with plenty of opportunities for customizing.

Tools
The Necessities (pages 11–12)
9 x 6-in (23 x 15-cm) metal brownie pan
Baby Onesie template (see Templates, page 115)
Stitching tool (see Resources, page 114)
Cake decorating tips: #2, #2A, #10

Ingredients
One 16-oz (455-g) box cake mix (any flavor) prepared, or batter for one 9-in (23-cm) cake
1 recipe Vanilla Frosting (page 17) or 1 container store-bought frosting
8 oz (225 g) white fondant (see Resources, page 114)
1 cup Royal Icing (page 17)
Pink, blue, or your choice of gel food coloring

Bake the cake
1 Preheat oven to 350°F (180°C). Prepare the cake batter. Spray the brownie pan with non-stick spray.

2 Pour the batter into the pan, filling it three-quarters full. Smooth the top and bake for 20–30 minutes, or until the top springs back when lightly pressed and a toothpick inserted into the center comes out clean.

3 Place the pan on a wire rack to cool for about 10 minutes. If the cake rose above the pan, use a serrated knife to cut away the top of the cake to make it level (set the knife across the top of the pan so you can use it as a guide). Run a knife around the edge to loosen the sides. Invert the cake out of the pan onto a wire rack and allow to finish cooling. When completely cool, wrap in plastic wrap and freeze for at least two hours until cold and firm.

Prepare to decorate
1 Tint 6 oz (170 g) white fondant the desired base color. (See tinting instructions on page 16.) Wrap tightly with plastic wrap until ready to use.

2 Tint the remaining 2 oz (55 g) white fondant a darker shade of the base color for the polka dots. Wrap tightly in plastic wrap until ready to use.

3 Attach a #2 cake decorating tip to a piping bag. Fill the bag with white royal icing.

Cut the cake
1 Remove cake from the freezer and unwrap. Place on a piece of parchment.

2 Place template on top of the cake and use a sharp knife to cut out the cake, using the template as the guide. Use the knife to clean up any rough edges on the cakelet.

3 Using a tapered angled spatula, crumb coat the cakelet with Vanilla Frosting starting around the sides of the cake and finishing on the top. Use enough frosting so that the spatula doesn't come into direct contact with the cake. This will keep you from dislodging too many crumbs.

Cover the cakelet
1 Dust a clean, dry work surface with

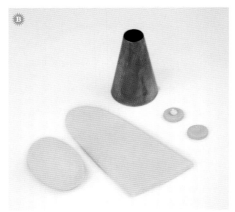

Level *Easy*
Batter yields enough cake for *3 cakelets*
Fondant quantity listed is suitable to complete *1 cakelet*

cornstarch. Roll out the base color fondant into a circle that's $\frac{1}{4}$ in (6 mm) thick.

2 Slide your hands underneath the fondant using open palms so as to not poke a hole in it. Pick the fondant up and lay it over the cakelet. Smooth the top of the cakelet first, using an open palm. Then smooth the fondant down over the sides of the cakelet. Use your pastry wheel to cut away excess fondant around the bottom of the cakelet.

3 Gently roll out a gumball-sized ball of the excess base-color fondant into a flat oval $\frac{1}{4}$ in (6 mm) thick to create the flap.

4 Use a paintbrush to dab the backside of the flap with water. Place on the bottom of the onesie, using the photograph to the right as a guide.

Finishing touches

1 Use your quilting tool to add a stitching effect around the legs, arms and neck of the onesie.

2 Dust a clean, dry work surface with cornstarch. Roll out the darker colored fondant until it's $\frac{1}{8}$ in (3 mm) thick.

3 Use the small circle cutters or #2A decorating tip to cut out eight to ten circles (if the circles get stuck in the tip, use the end of a paintbrush to push them out).

4 With the paintbrush, dab water on the onesie wherever you want to have polka dots.

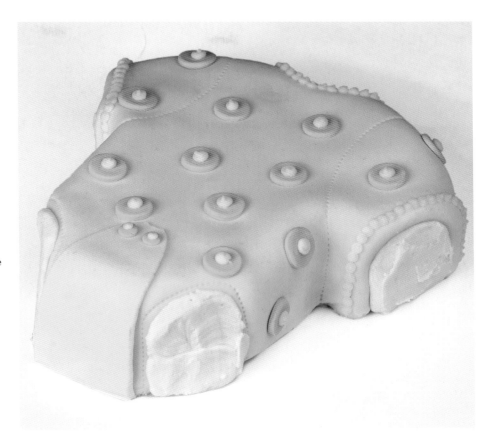

Press the darker toned pink circles on top.

5 Use the #10 tip to cut out two circles to make the snaps on the onesie flap. Adhere with water.

6 Using the piping bag filled with white royal icing and a #2 tip, pipe dots on the darker toned circles and also around the arms and neck of the onesie.

7 Change the #2 tip from the royal icing piping bag to the #10 tip.

8 Pipe royal icing to fill in the areas where the legs and arms would be.

Now I Know My ABCs

My sons loved playing with baby blocks, stacking and knocking them over again and again. As they learned their letters, they would try to spell their names or the names of our pets using the blocks. How cute, right? As they got a little older, though, the blocks became flying projectiles. I can't say I miss *that* stage.

Tools

One 9 x 13-in (23 x 33-cm) cake pan
The Necessities (pages 11–12)
¾-in (1.8-cm) circle cutter
1½-in (3.75-cm) scalloped circle cutter
Letter presses
Fondant smoothers
Ruler

Ingredients

One 16-oz (455-g) box cake mix (any flavor)
  prepared, or batter for one 9-in (23-cm) cake
1 recipe Vanilla Frosting (page 17) or 1
  container store-bought frosting
1 lb (455 g) white fondant (see Resources,
  page 114)
Lime green, leaf green, and pink gel food
  coloring

Bake the cake

1 Preheat oven to 350°F (180°C). Spray the cake pan with non-stick spray. Fill the pan three-quarters full with batter. Bake for 30–45 minutes, or until the top springs back when lightly pressed and a toothpick inserted into the center comes out clean.

2 Allow the cake to cool for a few minutes in the pan. If the cake rose above the pan, use a serrated knife to cut away the top to make it level (set the knife across the top of the pan so you can use it as a guide). Run a knife around the edge to loosen the sides. Invert the cake out of the pan and place on a wire rack to finish cooling. When completely cool, wrap in plastic wrap and freeze at least two hours until cold and firm.

Prepare to decorate

1 Tint 8 oz (225 g) of the fondant with a mixture of lime green and leaf green gel food coloring. Tint another 4 oz (115 g) with the pink gel food coloring. (See tinting instructions on page 16.) Leave 4 oz (115 g) untinted.

2 Remove the cake from the freezer and unwrap. Cut out two 3-in (7.5-cm) squares of cake. Use a ruler to make sure your blocks are exactly square.

3 Place one of the cakes on a piece of parchment. Using a tapered angled spatula, apply a smooth layer of Vanilla Frosting on top.

Level *Easy*
Batter yields enough cake for *4 cakelets*
Fondant quantity listed is suitable to complete *1 cakelet*

Set the other cake square on top of the first one. Use a ruler to be sure the cakelet is exactly 3 in (7.5 cm) high. If necessary, add or remove frosting (or trim cake) to make the square the right size. ☀

4 Using a tapered angled spatula, apply a smooth crumb coat of Vanilla Frosting to the sides of the cakelet. Use enough frosting so that the spatula doesn't come into direct contact with the cake. This will keep you from dislodging too many crumbs. Do not ice the top.

Cover the cakelet

1 Dust a clean, dry work surface with cornstarch. Roll out 8 oz (225 g) of green fondant into a sheet $\frac{1}{4}$ in (6 mm) thick and large enough to generously cover the block.

2 Slide your hand under the fondant to lift and gently lay it on top of the cakelet. Use your hands to smooth the top, then the sides of the cakelet. Use two fondant smoothers to gently press and smooth the opposite sides of the cake at the same time, until you've smoothed all sides and have clean edges.

3 Use a pastry wheel to cut away the excess fondant.

Finishing touches

1 Roll out 2 oz (55 g) of the pink fondant into a strip $\frac{1}{8}$ in (3 mm) thick, $\frac{1}{2}$ in (1.25 cm) wide, and 10 in (25.5 cm) long. Adhere the strip to the bottom of the block using a paintbrush and water.

2 Dust a clean, dry work surface with cornstarch. Roll out the white fondant into a sheet $\frac{1}{8}$ in (3 mm) thick. Cut out five scalloped circles with the cutter. ☀

3 Use a small ball tool to add a circular indent in each bump of the scalloped edge.

4 Brush a little water onto the top and sides of each block and adhere the scalloped circles. Be sure to center them.

5 Dust a clean, dry work surface with cornstarch. Roll the remaining pink fondant into a sheet $\frac{1}{8}$ in (3 mm) thick. Use the letter presses to imprint five letters on the fondant. Center and cut out the letters using the $\frac{3}{4}$-in (1.8-cm) circle cutter.

6 Brush a little water onto the scalloped circles and adhere the letter circles.

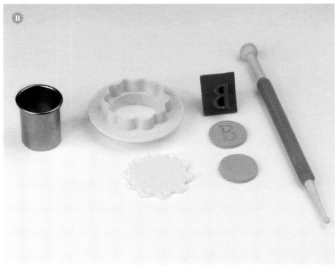

Xylophone Toy

I used to love this toy when I was a kid. I'd spend hours trying to tap out my favorite tunes. Considering all the time I spent with it, I guess it's not all that surprising that I ended up earning my college degree in classical music performance. Even a toy this simple can inspire a lifelong love of music!

Tools

9 x 6-in (23 x 15-cm) metal brownie pan
The Necessities (pages 11–12)
Xylophone template (see Templates, page 115)
$\frac{3}{4}$-in (1.8-cm) circle cutter
$1\frac{1}{2}$-in (3.75-cm) circle cutter
Fondant smoother

Ingredients

One 16-oz (455-g) box cake mix (any flavor)
** prepared, or batter for one 9-in (23-cm) cake**
1 recipe Vanilla Frosting (page 17) or
** 1 container store-bought icing**
2 lbs (910 g) white fondant
** (see resources, page 114)**
4 oz (115 g) red fondant
** (see resources, page 114)**
Gel food colorings: orange, yellow, green,
** blue, purple**
4 oz (115 g) black fondant

Bake the cake

1 Preheat oven to 350°F (180°C). Prepare the cake batter. Spray the brownie pan with non-stick spray.

2 Pour the batter into the pan, filling it three-quarters of the way full. Smooth the top and bake for 20–30 minutes, or until the top springs back when lightly pressed and a toothpick inserted into the center comes out clean.

3 Place pan on a wire rack to cool for about 10 minutes. If the cake rose above the pan, use a serrated knife to cut away the top of the cake to make it level (set the knife across the top of the pan so you can use it as a guide). Run a knife around the edge to loosen the sides. Invert the cake out of the pan onto a wire rack and allow to finish cooling. When completely cool, wrap in plastic wrap and freeze for at least two hours until cold and firm.

Prepare to decorate

1 Divide 1 lb (455 g) of white fondant into four 3 oz (85 g) portions, and one 4 oz (115 g) portion. Following the tinting instructions on page 16, use the gel food coloring to tint each 3 oz (85 g) portion one of the following colors: orange, yellow, green, and purple. Color the 4 oz (115 g) portion of fondant light blue. You will be using pre-colored fondant for the colors red and black. Individually wrap each color in plastic wrap until ready to use.

2 Remove cake from the freezer and unwrap. Use a serrated knife to cut along the both long sides of the cake so that the cake narrows slightly at one end. Use the knife to clean up any rough edges of the cakelet.

3 Place cakelet on a piece of parchment. Using a tapered angled spatula, crumb coat the cakelet with Vanilla Frosting, starting

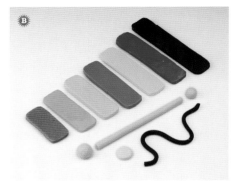

at the sides and finishing at the top. Use enough frosting so that the spatula doesn't come into direct contact with the cake. This will keep you from dislodging too many crumbs.

Covering the cakelet

1 Dust a clean, dry work surface with cornstarch. Roll out 8 oz (230 g) of white fondant until it is $\frac{1}{4}$ in (6 mm) thick and large enough to cover the entire cakelet.

2 Slide your hand under the fondant, lift it up, and gently place onto the cakelet. Use an

Level *Easy/Intermediate*
Batter yields enough cake for *1 cakelet*
Fondant quantity listed is suitable to complete *1 cakelet*

open palm to smooth the top of the cakelet first, then the sides. Use a pastry wheel to cut away excess fondant around the base.

3 Use the large ball tool to press an indented line $\frac{1}{4}$ in (6 mm) from the top, going all the way around the sides of the cake.

4 Use a small ball tool to indent a line that runs evenly down the center of the top of the cake.

Assemble

1 Dust a clean, dry work surface with cornstarch. Working with one color at a time, roll out each piece of fondant until it is $\frac{1}{4}$ in (6 mm) thick. Use the templates to cut out the different bars in rainbow order, using the biggest one for the black fondant and the smallest one for the red. ✺

2 Adhere the bars to the top of the cakelet using a few dabs of water.

3 Roll out approximately 5 oz (145 g) of white fondant $\frac{1}{4}$ in (6 mm) thick. Use a $\frac{3}{4}$-in (1.8-cm) circle cutter to cut out two circles per xylophone bar, for a total of fourteen circles.

4 Adhere the circles to each end of the xylophone bars with a little water.

5 Roll out the remaining red fondant into a sheet $\frac{1}{2}$ in (1.25 cm) thick and use the $1\frac{1}{2}$-in (3.75-cm) circle cutter to cut out the four wheels of the xylophone toy. Adhere to the base of the cakelet using a little water.

Finishing touches

1 Start to construct the mallet by rolling out a log of blue fondant that is $\frac{1}{4}$ in (6 mm) wide.

2 Roll out two balls of blue fondant, one slightly larger than the other.

3 Roll a thin log of black fondant to make the string. Use a fondant smoother to create an evenly thin line.

4 Place the blue fondant mallet onto the cakeboard. Adhere the two blue balls to each end using a dab of water.

5 Adhere one end of the black fondant "string" to the small ball on the mallet.

6 Attach the other end the string to xylophone cakelet by using a standard ball tool to create an indent in the front of the xylophone. Adhere the black fondant string into the indent with a dab of water.

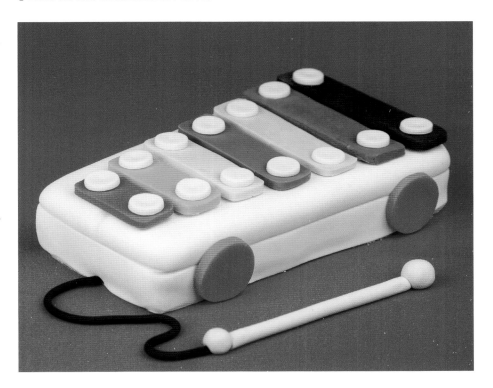

Baby Bottle

Nothing signifies babyhood better than a baby bottle. Just looking at one conjures up images of cuddling a fuzzy-headed, good-smelling little newborn sleepily sipping a warm bottle. It's the perfect cakelet for new moms and moms-to-be—even new grandmas—and the design is incredibly easy.

Tools

One 9 x 13-in (23 x 33-cm) cake pan
The Necessities (pages 11–12)
3-in (7.5-cm) circle cutter
2-in (5-cm) circle cutter
Flower cutter
Fondant smoothers
Toothpick

Ingredients

One 16-oz (455-g) box cake mix (any flavor) prepared, or batter for one 9-in (23-cm) cake
1 recipe Vanilla Frosting (page 17) or 1 container store-bought frosting
1 lb (455 g) white fondant (see Resources, page 114)
Orange and blue gel food colorings

Bake the cake

1 Preheat oven to 350°F (180°C). Prepare the cake batter. Spray the cake pan with non-stick spray.

2 Pour the batter into the pan, filling it three-quarters full. Smooth the top and bake for 25 minutes, or until the top springs back when lightly pressed and a toothpick inserted into the center comes out clean.

3 Place pan on a wire rack to cool for about 10 minutes. If the cake rose above the pan, use a serrated knife to cut away the top of the cake to make it level (set the knife across the top of the pan so you can use it as a guide). Run a knife around the edge to loosen the sides. Invert the cake out of the pan onto a wire rack and allow it to finish cooling. When completely cool, wrap in plastic wrap and freeze for at least two hours until cold and firm.

Prepare the cakelet

1 Remove cake from the freezer and unwrap. Use the 3-in (7.5-cm) circle cutter to cut out two round cakes. ✸

2 Place one of the round cakes on a piece of parchment. Using a tapered angled spatula, apply a smooth layer of Vanilla Frosting on top. Set the other round cake on top of the first one to make a stack about 4 in (10 cm) tall. Use a knife to round the edges on the top cake. Then use your fingers to brush away any rough edges.

Level *Easy*
Batter yields enough cake for *4 cakelets*
Fondant quantity listed is suitable to complete *1 cakelet*

3 Place the cakelet on a piece of parchment. Using a tapered angled spatula, crumb coat the cakelet with Vanilla Frosting, starting at the sides and finishing at the top. Use enough frosting so that the spatula doesn't come into direct contact with the cake. This will keep you from dislodging too many crumbs.

Prepare to decorate

Follow the tinting instructions on page 16 to tint 6 oz (170 g) of fondant light blue, and 2 oz (55 g) orange. Wrap each color individually in plastic wrap until ready to use.

Cover the cakelet

1 Dust a clean, dry work surface with cornstarch. Roll out 8 oz (225 g) of white fondant into a sheet $\frac{1}{4}$ in (6 mm) thick 8 in (20.5 cm) long and 4 in (10 cm) wide.

2 Wrap the fondant sheet around the cakelet and use an X-Acto knife to cut away the excess at the seam. Use two fondant smoothers to smooth the top and sides of

the cake. Use a pastry wheel to cut away any excess around the base.

3 Place the cakelet in the refrigerator to chill for 30 minutes.

Assemble

1 Dust a clean, dry work surface with cornstarch. Roll out a piece of the blue fondant into a sheet $\frac{1}{4}$ in (6 mm) thick. Use the 3-in (7.5-cm) circle cutter to cut out a circle.

2 Roll a piece of the blue fondant into a sheet 1 in (2.5 cm) thick. Use the 2-in (5-cm) circle cutter to cut out a circle.

3 Mold a piece of fondant the size of a ping-pong ball into a shape for the nipple.

4 Use a little water to adhere the blue fondant nipple to the thick 2-in (5-cm) circle, then adhere that to the 3-in (7.5-cm) circle. Adhere the blue fondant bottle top assembly to the top of the cake.

Finishing touches

1 Roll out 4 oz (115 g) of orange fondant into a sheet $\frac{1}{8}$ in (3 mm) thick. Use the flower cutter to cut out ten to twelve flowers.

2 Adhere the orange flowers around the side of the bottle.

3 Roll and flatten ten to twelve pearl-sized circles of white fondant and use a dab of water to adhere one to the center of each orange flower. Stipple with the toothpick.

Chapter 6

Macho Macho Man

Play Ball!

Baseball fans of all ages would love to receive this cakelet, but what about soccer addicts, hoops heads and golf junkies? No problem. It's easy to alter this design to create different kinds of balls. Just search the web for images of those iconic balls to use as your model.

Tools
6-cavity Wilton mini ball pan
The Necessities (pages 11–12)
Piping bag
Cake decorating tip #2

Ingredients
One 16-oz (455-g) box cake mix (any flavor) prepared, or batter for one 9-in (23-cm) cake
1 recipe Vanilla Frosting (page 17) or 1 container store-bought frosting
1 lb (455 g) white fondant (see Resources, page 114)
1 recipe Royal Icing (page 17)
Red gel food coloring

Bake the cakes
1 Preheat oven to 350°F (180°C). Spray each of the mini ball cavities to be used with non-stick spray (you will need two mini ball cakes for each cakelet). Fill each cavity to be used three-quarters full with batter. Bake for 10–12 minutes, or until the tops spring back when lightly pressed and a toothpick inserted into the center comes out clean.

2 Allow the cakes to cool for a few minutes in the pan. If the cakes are domed, use a serrated knife to trim the cakes until they are level (use the top of the pan as your guide). Run a knife around the edge to loosen the

sides. Invert the cakes out of the pan onto a wire rack to finish cooling. When completely cool, wrap each in plastic and freeze for at least two hours until cold and firm.

Prepare the cakelet
1 Remove cakes from the freezer and unwrap. Place two cakes flat-side down on a piece of parchment and cut away any hard edges.

2 Using a tapered angled spatula, apply a layer of Vanilla Frosting to the bottom of one of the ball cakes. Adhere the bottom of another cake to it to form a sphere.

3 Cut away any rough edges where the two halves meet to make a smooth seam. Cut out a wedge from the sphere so that the cakelet can sit flat.

4 Using a tapered angled spatula, crumb coat the cakelet with Vanilla Frosting. Use enough frosting so that the spatula doesn't come into direct contact with the cake. This will keep you from dislodging too many crumbs.

Cover the cakelet
1 Dust a clean, dry work surface with cornstarch. Roll out $5\frac{1}{2}$ oz (160 g) of white fondant into a circle $\frac{1}{4}$ in (6 mm) thick and no larger than a dinner plate.

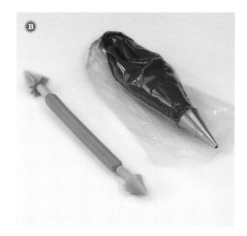

Level *Easy*
Batter yields enough cake for *3 cakelets*
Fondant quantity listed is suitable to complete *1 cakelet*

2 Slide your hand under the fondant, lift it up, and gently place it on top of a cakelet. Smooth it down and around the cake.

3 Cut away excess fondant around the base with a pastry wheel.

4 Place the cakelet in the refrigerator to chill for 30 minutes.

Finishing touches

1 Remove the fondant-covered cakelet from the refrigerator. Use a fondant marking tool to outline the impression of a seam on the baseball.

2 Color the Royal Icing with red gel food coloring.

3 Fit the #2 tip onto the piping bag and fill it with the red icing. ⓑ Pipe small Vs all along the impressed seam path, as illustrated in the photo to the left.

Corner-Office Briefcase

To most, a briefcase signifies importance. But when I see them, I like to think they're filled with candy, whoopee cushions and fake mustaches instead of boring old files. Who says business has to be so serious anyway?

Tools

9 x 6-in (23 x 15-cm) metal brownie pan
The Necessities (pages 11–12)
Toothpick
Fondant smoothers
Ruler

Ingredients

One 16-oz (455-g) box cake mix (any flavor)
** prepared, or batter for one 9-in (23-cm) cake**
1 recipe Vanilla Frosting (page 17) or
** 1 container store-bought frosting**
1 lb (455 g) chocolate fondant
** (see Resources, page 114)**
3 oz (85 g) black fondant
** (see Resources, page 114)**
Gold luster dust
1 teaspoon vodka

Make the handle (2–3 days prior to decorating)

1 Dust a clean dry work surface with cornstarch. Roll out a thin log of black fondant until it is $\frac{1}{4}$ in (6 mm) thick and 2 in (5 cm) long.

2 Bend the log into the shape of a square "U" to create a handle. Place on a piece of parchment and set aside to dry out for at least two days at room temperature out of direct sunlight (to keep the color from fading).

Bake the cake

1 Preheat oven to 350°F (180°C). Prepare the cake batter. Spray the brownie pan with non-stick spray.

2 Pour the batter into the pan, filling it three-quarters full. Smooth the top and bake for 20–30 minutes, or until the top springs back when lightly pressed and a toothpick inserted into the center comes out clean.

3 Place the pan on a wire rack to cool for about 10 minutes. If the cake rose above the pan, use a serrated knife to cut away the top of the cake to make it level (set the knife across the top of the pan so you can use it as a guide). Run a knife around the edge to loosen the sides. Invert the cake out of the pan onto a wire rack and allow it to finish cooling. When completely cool, wrap in plastic wrap and freeze for at least two hours until cold and firm.

Prepare to decorate

1 Remove cake from the freezer and unwrap. Use a serrated knife to cut it in half to make two $4\frac{1}{2}$ x 6-in (11.25 x 15-cm) rectangles. Place one on a piece of parchment, and reserve the other for another use. ✹

2 Using a tapered angled spatula, crumb coat the cakelet with Vanilla Frosting. Use enough frosting so that the spatula doesn't come into direct contact with the cake. This will keep you from dislodging too many crumbs.

Cover the cakelet

1 Dust a clean, dry work surface with cornstarch. Roll out 12 oz (340 g) of the chocolate fondant into a sheet $\frac{1}{4}$ in (6 mm) thick.

2 Slide your hand under the fondant, lift it up, and gently lay it on top of a cakelet. Use your hands to smooth the fondant over the top and then down around the corners and sides. Use two fondant smoothers to further smooth the top and sides of the cake.

3 Cut away excess fondant with a pastry wheel.

Assemble

1 Use a fondant marking tool or the side of a ruler to press a long, straight line around the vertical sides of the briefcase, about a third of the way from the top of the cakelet. This will create the appearance that the briefcase has a closed lid.

2 Dust a clean, dry work surface with cornstarch. Roll out 4 oz (115 g) of the chocolate

Level *Easy*
Batter yields enough cake for *2 cakelets*
Fondant quantity listed is suitable to complete *1 cakelet*

fondant into two strips approximately 8 in (20.5 cm) long and ½ in (1.25 cm) wide to create the decorative borders.

3 Use a small ball tool to add some texture to the strips. (You can also use a texture sheet.)

4 Brush a little water on the edges of the briefcase where you will be adhering the strips. Attach the strips up the front, over the top and down the back of the briefcase.

5 Cut away the excess fondant.

6 Use the fondant marking tool or a ruler to indent the strips in the front and back of the briefcase to match the line in the fondant underneath.

Finishing touches

Front plates

1 Dust a clean, dry work surface with cornstarch. Roll out chocolate fondant until it is ¼ in (6 mm) thick. Cut out two rectangles that are ¾ in (1.8 cm) long by ½ in (1.25 cm) wide.

2 Brush a little water onto the front of the briefcase inside the fondant straps and below the indentation. Adhere the rectangles.

3 Roll two small pieces of chocolate fondant into two balls and press them onto the rectangle.

4 Use your fondant marking tool or a toothpick to indent a small line in the rectangle to make the key holes.

Latches

1 Roll out two small balls of chocolate fondant and press them onto the briefcase just above the crease and above the top inside corners of the rectangles.

2 Roll out two thin chocolate fondant logs to make the latches for the brief case.

3 Brush a little water on the circles and attach the latches. They should go over the crease and onto the rectangle below.

4 Use the marking tool to add a crease to the top of the latch for a hinge detail.

Handle

1 Roll out 2 oz (55 g) of the black fondant until it is ¼ in (6 mm) thick. Cut out two small rectangles and adhere them with a little water to the front of the briefcase where the handle will be attached.

2 Gently press the black fondant handle into the rectangles to mark where the handle will be inserted.

3 Use a ball tool to push into the marked spaces. Gently insert your briefcase handle into the cake.

Gold paint

In a small bowl, mix a small amount of gold luster dust with vodka (it should be the consistency of thick gravy). Brush the front briefcase details with the gold luster paint until well coated.

High Roller

Level *Easy*
Batter yields enough cake for *3 cakelets*
Fondant quantity listed is suitable to complete *1 cakelet*

Bachelor parties, game night, a James Bond film fest in your living room—this super-simple cakelet is just the thing to get the party started. Anyone who loves Vegas or games of chance won't be able resist it.

Tools
The Necessities (pages 11–12)
One 9 x 13-in (23 x 33-cm) cake pan
¾-in (1.8-cm) circle cutter
Fondant smoothers
Ruler

Ingredients
One 16-oz (455-g) box cake mix (any flavor)
   prepared, or batter for one 9-in (23-cm) cake
1 recipe Vanilla Frosting (page 17) or
   1 container store-bought frosting
1 lb (455 g) white fondant
   (see Resources, page 114)
8 oz (225 g) black fondant
   (see Resources, page 114)

Bake the cake
1 Preheat oven to 350°F (180°C). Spray the cake pan with non-stick spray. Fill three-quarters full with batter. Bake for 30-45 minutes, or until the top springs back when lightly pressed and a toothpick inserted into the center comes out clean.

2 Allow the cake to cool for a few minutes in the pan. If the cake rose above the pan, use a serrated knife to cut away the top to make it level (set the knife across the top of the pan so you can use it as a guide). Run a knife around the edge to loosen the sides. Invert the cake out of the pan and onto a wire rack to finish cooling. When completely cool, wrap in

plastic wrap and freeze for at least two hours until cold and firm.

Prepare to decorate
1 Remove cake from the freezer and unwrap. Cut out two 4-in (10-cm) squares of cake.

2 Place a cake on a piece of parchment. Using a tapered angled spatula, apply a smooth layer of Vanilla Frosting on top. Set the other cake square on top of the frosted square. Use a ruler to be sure the cube is exactly 4 in (10 cm) high. If necessary, add or remove frosting (or trim cake) to form a 4-in (10-cm) cube.

3 Using a tapered angled spatula, apply a smooth crumb coat of Vanilla Frosting to the sides of the cakes. Use enough frosting so that the spatula doesn't come into direct contact with the cake. This will keep you from dislodging too many crumbs. Do not ice the top.

Cover the cakelet
1 Dust a clean, dry work surface with cornstarch. Roll out 1 lb (455 g) of white fondant into a sheet ¼ in (6 mm) thick and large enough to generously cover the cakelet.

2 Slide your hand under the fondant, lift it up, and gently lay it on top of the cakelet. Use your hands to smooth the top first, then

smooth the fondant down the sides of the cakelet. Use two fondant smoothers to gently press and smooth the opposite sides of the cake at the same time, until you've smoothed all sides and have clean edges.

3 Use a pastry wheel to cut away excess fondant.

Finishing Touches
1 Dust a clean, dry work surface with cornstarch. Roll out 8 oz (225 g) of black fondant into a sheet ¼ in (6 mm) thick.

2 Using a small circle cutter, cut out twenty-one black dots.

3 Use a little water to adhere the dots to the top and sides of the cakes in configurations you would see on dice.

Fore!

Sure, you can give the golfer in your life a practical gift set complete with spare balls, tees, and a ball marker. But it's a little predictable, isn't it? If you really want to make them smile, wrap up this edible version instead.

Tools

One 9 x 6-in (23 x 15-cm) metal brownie pan
The Necessities (pages 11–12)
Toothpick
Fondant smoothers
Golf Ball Marker template (see Templates, page 115)
Spoon
Small circle cutter

Ingredients

One 16-oz (455-g) box cake mix (any flavor) prepared, or batter for one 9-in (23-cm) cake
1 recipe Vanilla Frosting (page 17) or 1 container store-bought frosting
8 oz (225 g) chocolate or brown fondant (see Resources, page 114)
1 lb (455 g) green fondant (see Resources, page 114)
8 oz (225 g) white fondant (see Resources, page 114)
Black gel food coloring
1 teaspoon vodka
Silver luster dust

Make the golf ball marker (two days prior to decorating)

1 Tint 2 oz (55 g) of white fondant with a drop of black gel food coloring to create gray fondant.

2 Roll out a handful of the gray fondant into a rectangle ¼ in (6 mm) thick. Cut out the ball marker with an X-Acto knife, using the Golf Ball Marker template as a guide.

3 Use a small circle cutter to make a decorative indent in the ball marker. ⚙

4 Place the ball marker on a piece of parchment and set aside to dry for at least two days at room temperature.

Bake the cake

1 Preheat oven to 350°F (180°C). Prepare the cake batter. Spray the brownie pan with non-stick spray.

2 Pour the batter into the pan, filling it three-quarters full. Smooth the top and bake for 20–30 minutes, or until the top springs back when lightly pressed and a toothpick inserted into the center comes out clean.

3 Place the pan on a wire rack to cool for about 10 minutes. If the cake rose above the pan, use a serrated knife to cut away the top of the cake

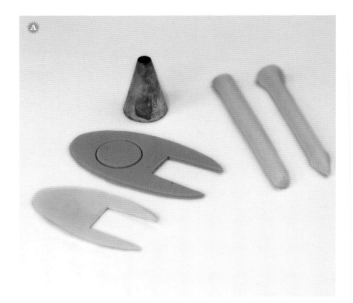

Level *Intermediate*
Batter yields enough cake for *1 cakelet*
Fondant quantity listed is suitable to complete *1 cakelet*

to make it level (set the knife across the top of the pan so you can use it as a guide). Run a knife around the edge to loosen the sides. Invert the cake out of the pan onto a wire rack and allow it to finish cooling. When completely cool, wrap in plastic wrap and freeze for at least two hours until cold and firm.

Prepare to decorate

1 Remove cake from the freezer and unwrap. Place on a piece of parchment bottom side up.

2 Use a spoon to scoop out two golf ball-sized cups where the golf balls will be placed. 🌀

3 Use a knife to cut out a shallow rectangular well where the golf tees will be placed.

4 Use a spoon to carve out a shallow rounded rectangular well where the ball marker will be placed.

5 Using a tapered angled spatula, crumb coat the cakelet with Vanilla Frosting, starting at the sides and finishing at the top. Use enough frosting so that the spatula doesn't come into direct contact with the cake. This will keep you from dislodging too many crumbs.

Assemble

1 Dust a clean, dry work surface with cornstarch. Roll out the green fondant until it is $\frac{1}{4}$ in (6 mm) thick and large enough to cover the entire cake.

2 Slide your hand under the fondant, lift it up, and gently lay it on top of the cakelet. Use

your fingers to gently contour the fondant over the carved-out areas on the top of the cake. Cut away the excess fondant with a pastry wheel.

3 Roll out the chocolate or brown fondant into a strip approximately $1\frac{1}{2}$ in (3.75 cm) wide.

4 Lightly brush water on all four sides of the cake. Wrap the brown strip around the cake, making sure the seam ends up in a back corner.

Finishing touches

Golf balls

1 Roll two equally sized pieces of white fondant into golf-ball-sized balls. Place them in the two contoured areas on the top of the cake.

2 Use a small ball tool to poke indentations all over the white balls to create the dimpled texture of a golf ball.

Golf tees

1 Roll out two $2\frac{1}{4}$ in (5.75 cm) white fondant logs.

2 Gently flare one end of each log to make the top of the golf tee. Sharpen a point on the opposite ends.

3 Place the golf tees in the rectangular recess on the top of the cake.

Ball marker

1 Place the dry fondant ball marker inside the last open contoured recess.

2 In a small bowl, mix a small amount of silver luster dust with vodka (it should be the consistency of thick gravy). Paint the ball marker with the mixture until well coated.

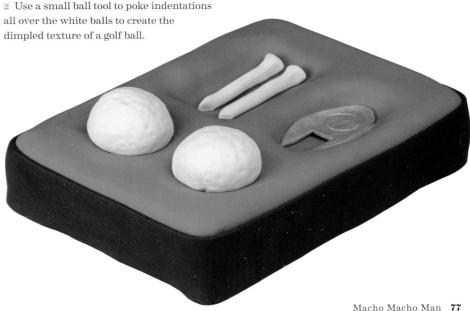

Cask Me Anything

I know plenty of wine, spirit, and beer lovers who would be thrilled to receive an entire barrel of their favorite beverage. Although price and logistics make a gift of that scale pretty near impossible, this sweet little cakelet lets them know it's the thought that counts.

Tools

6-cavity Wilton king-size muffin pan
The Necessities (pages 11–12)
Toothpick
Wood-grain texture sheet
2½-in (6.25-cm) circle cutter

Ingredients

One 16-oz (455-g) box cake mix (any flavor) prepared, or batter for one 9-in (23-cm) cake
1 recipe Vanilla Frosting (page 17) or 1 container store bought frosting
1 lb (455 g) chocolate or brown fondant (see Resources, page 114)

Bake the cakes

1 Preheat oven to 350°F (180°C). Spray each of the king-size muffin pan cavities to be used with non-stick spray (you will need two muffin cakes for each cakelet). Fill the cavities being used three-quarters full with batter. Bake for 25 minutes, or until the tops spring back when lightly pressed and a toothpick inserted into the center comes out clean.

2 Allow cakes to cool for a few minutes in the pan. Run a knife around the edges to loosen the sides. Invert the cakes out of the pan onto a wire rack to finish cooling. When completely cool, wrap each in plastic wrap and freeze for at least two hours until cold and firm.

Prepare the cakelet

1 Slice ½ in (1.25 cm) off the top (the wide end) of each muffin.

2 Place a muffin cake right side up on a piece of parchment. Using a tapered angled spatula, apply a layer of Vanilla Frosting to the top. Place another cake upside down on top of it, so that the wider ends are together and they form an oblong barrel shape.

3 Cut away any uneven edges where the two halves meet to make a smooth seam. Cut a shallow wedge from the area where the cakes meet, so that the barrel will sit flat when turned on its side. ☀

4 Using a tapered angled spatula, crumb coat the cakelet with Vanilla Frosting. Use enough frosting so that the spatula doesn't

Level *Intermediate*
Batter yields enough cake for *3 cakelets*
Fondant quantity listed is suitable to complete *1 cakelet*

come into direct contact with the cake. This will keep you from dislodging too many crumbs.

Cover the cakelet

1 Dust a clean, dry work surface with cornstarch. Roll out 8 oz (225 g) of chocolate or brown fondant into a circle $\frac{1}{4}$ in (6 mm) thick.

2 Press the wood-grain texture sheet into it to emboss it with a wood-grain effect.

3 Use the circle cutter to cut out two circles to use for each end of the barrel.  Adhere them to the sides of the barrel.

4 Dust a clean, dry work surface with cornstarch. Roll out 8 oz (225 g) of chocolate or brown fondant into a circle $\frac{1}{4}$ in (6 mm) thick.

5 Press the wood-grain texture sheet into it to emboss it with a wood-grain effect.

6 Slide your hand under the fondant, lift it up, and gently place it on top of the cakelet. Gently smooth the fondant over the cake, being careful not to smooth away the textured effect.

7 Use an X-Acto knife to cut away the excess fondant at the ends of the barrel. Use a pastry wheel to cut away excess fondant from the base of the barrel.

8 Place the cakelet in the refrigerator to chill for 30 minutes.

Finishing touches

1 Dust a clean, dry work surface with cornstarch. Roll out 4 oz (115 g) of chocolate or brown fondant into a sheet $\frac{1}{8}$ in (3 mm) thick.

2 Use your pastry wheel to cut two strips of fondant $\frac{3}{4}$ in (1.8 cm) wide and 10 in (25.5 cm) long for the bands around the barrel.

3 Lightly brush water around the barrel and adhere the strips. Cut away any excess fondant.

4 Use the flower veining tool to create wood-grain impressions along both sides of each strip.

Additional decorating ideas

Use a piping bag filled with royal icing (page 17) and #2 cake decorating tip to write your favorite brand of beverage on the barrel, or personalize it with the recipient's name. Instead of piping the age of the wine, pipe their date of birth for a truly custom creation.

Have a Cigar

We play poker at our house almost every Saturday night. The usual characters show up with their lucky card protectors, sunflower seeds, coolers of libations and, of course, cigars. My husband sits at the head of the poker table, with his best poker face and a fat cigar hanging out of his mouth. It's the only time he has a cigar, and if he won more often, I'd say it was his good luck charm.

Tools
9 x 6-in (23 x 15-cm) metal brownie pan
The Necessities (pages 11–12)
Toothpick
Fondant smoothers
Small flower cutter
Ruler

Ingredients
One 16-oz (455-g) box cake mix (any flavor)
  prepared, or batter for one 9-in (23-cm) cake
1 recipe Vanilla Frosting (page 17) or 1
  container store-bought frosting
1 lb (455 g) chocolate or brown fondant
1 oz (28 g) black fondant
1 lb (455 g) white fondant
1 oz (28 g) red fondant
  (see Resources, page 114)
Gold luster dust
Black petal dust
1 teaspoon vodka

Bake the cake
1 Preheat oven to 350°F (180°C). Prepare the cake batter. Spray the brownie pan with non-stick spray.

2 Pour the batter into the pan, filling it three-quarters full. Smooth the top and bake for 20–30 minutes, or until the top springs back when lightly pressed and a toothpick

inserted into the center comes out clean.

3 Place pan on a wire rack to cool for about 10 minutes. If the cake rose above the pan, use a serrated knife to cut away the top of the cake to make it level (set the knife across the top of the pan so you can use it as a guide). Run a knife around the edge to loosen the sides. Invert the cake out of the pan onto a wire rack and allow it to finish cooling. When completely cool, wrap in plastic wrap and freeze for at least two hours until cold and firm.

Prepare to decorate
1 Remove the cake from the freezer and unwrap. Use a serrated knife to cut it into an 8 x 6-in (20.5 x 15-cm) rectangle. ☀ Place on a piece of parchment.

2 Using a tapered angled spatula, crumb coat the cakelet with Vanilla Frosting, starting at the sides and finishing at the top. Use enough frosting so that the spatula doesn't come into direct contact with the cake. This will keep you from dislodging too many crumbs.

Cover the cakelet
1 Knead together 10 oz (290 g) of white fondant with 8 oz (225 g) of chocolate or brown fondant. Be sure not to over-knead the colors, as you want to see streaks of light and dark.

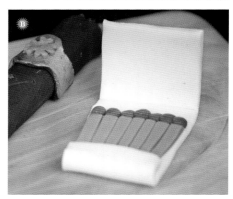

2 Dust a clean, dry work surface with cornstarch. Roll out the swirled fondant into a sheet $\frac{1}{4}$ in (6 mm) thick.

Level *Easy*
Batter yields enough cake for *1 cakelet*
Fondant quantity listed is suitable to complete *1 cakelet*

3 Slide your hand under the fondant, lift it up, and gently place it on top of the cakelet. Use your hands to smooth the fondant over the top and then around the corners and sides. Use two fondant smoothers to smooth the top and sides of the cake.

4 Cut away excess fondant with a pastry wheel, then roll out the scraps into a sheet $\frac{1}{8}$ in (3 mm) thick. Use the small flower cutter to cut out a flower for the label. Set aside for the final step.

Finishing touches

Create the impression of a lid

1 Using the side of a ruler, or a fondant marking tool, impress a horizontal line $\frac{1}{2}$ in (1.25 cm) from the top of the cakelet on the left and right sides. Continue the line across the front of the cake, connecting the two marked lines on the left and right.

2 Use a ball tool to create an indentation in the middle of the front of the box.

3 Use black petal dust and a small paint brush to lightly brush the crease of the box to give the seam the appearance of depth.

Make a matchbook

1 Knead together 2 oz (55 g) of white fondant and $\frac{1}{2}$ oz (14 g) of black fondant until they are blended well and uniformly gray in color.

2 Dust a clean, dry work surface with cornstarch. Roll out the light gray fondant into a sheet $\frac{1}{4}$ in (6 mm) thick. Cut out one $1\frac{1}{2}$-in (3.75-cm) square.

3 Use an X-Acto knife to cut vertical $\frac{3}{4}$-in-long (1.8 cm) "matches" in the square from the top to $\frac{1}{4}$ in (6 mm) from the bottom.

4 Dust the work surface with cornstarch and roll out 3 oz (85 g) of white fondant into a sheet $\frac{1}{4}$ in (6 mm) thick. Cut out one $3\frac{3}{4}$-in (9.35-cm) by $1\frac{3}{4}$-in (4.35-cm) rectangle.

5 Place the matches onto the white fondant rectangle $\frac{1}{2}$ in (1.25 cm) from the bottom. Adhere with water. Brush the base of the matches with water and fold the bottom of the white fondant over it.

6 Use the fondant marking tool to create two horizontal lines defining the crease in the cover of the matchbook.

7 Roll small balls of red fondant for the match heads and adhere them to the top of the gray matchsticks. Ⓑ

Make the cigar

1 Roll out a log of chocolate or brown fondant $5\frac{1}{2}$ in (13.75 cm) long and $\frac{3}{4}$ in (1.8 cm) thick.

2 Use a toothpick to poke multiple holes in one end of the roll.

3 Cut a strip of chocolate or brown fondant to wrap around the cigar for the label.

4 Affix the small light brown flower to the center of the label with a dab of water.

5 In a small bowl, combine gold luster dust with vodka (it should be the consistency of thick gravy) and paint the brown fondant label, leaving the flower unpainted.

6 Position the cigar and matchbox on top of the cigar box and adhere with water.

Chapter 7

Holidays

'Tis the Season

This is hands-down our most popular cakelet design during the holidays. Once you get comfortable with the process, the decorating options are endless, and you'll find yourself looking for excuses to make more. Don't just stick to traditional green and red, use bold colors, fun cutters, or pipe a monogram for that special teacher, friend or family member.

Tools
6-cavity mini ball pan
The Necessities (pages 11–12)
Stitching tool (see Resources, page 114)
Hook template (see Templates, page 115)
1-in (2.5-cm) circle cutter
3-in (7.5-cm) circle cutter
Flower cutter
Cake decorating tip #10
Toothpick

Ingredients
One 16-oz (455-g) box cake mix (any flavor)
  prepared, or batter for one 9-in (23-cm) cake
1 recipe Vanilla Frosting (page 17) or
  1 container store-bought frosting
8 oz (225 g) white fondant
  (see Resources, page 114)
4 oz (115 g) green fondant
  (see Resources, page 114)

Prepare the hook and button (two days prior to decorating)
1 Use the Hook template to trace a hook onto a piece of parchment paper. Turn the paper over (you should still be able to see the lines you drew). Roll 1 oz (28 g) of white fondant into a rope $\frac{1}{4}$ in (6 mm) thick and 3 in (7.5 cm) long. Using the lines as a guide, sculpt the rope into the shape of the hook. Allow to dry for 48 hours.

2 Dust a clean, dry work surface with cornstarch. Roll out 1 oz (28 g) of green fondant until $\frac{1}{8}$ in (3 mm) thick. Use the 1-in (2.5-cm) circle cutter to cut out a circle.

3 Using the wide end of a #10 tip, center it over the green circle and gently press to make an impression. With a ball tool (or a toothpick), make four depressions in the center of the green circle to give the impression of holes in a button. Place on parchment paper to dry for 48 hours.

Bake the cakes
1 Preheat oven to 350°F (180°C). Spray each of the mini ball cavities to be used with non-stick spray (you will need two mini ball cakes for one cakelet). Fill each cavity being used three-quarters full with batter. Bake for 10–12 minutes, or until the tops spring back when lightly pressed and a toothpick inserted into the center comes out clean.

2 Allow the cakes to cool for a few minutes in the pan. If the cakes are domed, use a serrated knife to trim the cakes until they are level (use the top of the pan as your guide). Run a knife around the edge to loosen the sides. Invert the cakes out of the pan onto a wire rack to finish cooling. When completely cool, wrap each in plastic

and freeze for at least two hours until cold and firm.

Prepare the cakelet
1 Place each cake flat side down on a piece of parchment and cut away any hard edges.

2 Using a tapered angled spatula, apply a layer of Vanilla Frosting to the bottom of one of the ball cakes. Adhere the bottom of another cake to it to form a sphere.

3 Cut away any rough edges where the two halves meet to make for a smooth seam. Cut out a wedge from the sphere so that the cakelet can sit flat.

Level *Intermediate*
Batter yields enough cake for *3 cakelets*
Fondant quantity listed is suitable to complete *1 cakelet*

4 Crumb coat the sphere with Vanilla Frosting. Use enough frosting so that the spatula doesn't come into direct contact with the cake. This will keep you from dislodging too many crumbs.

Cover the cakelet

1 Dust a clean, dry work surface with cornstarch. Roll out $5\frac{1}{2}$ oz (160 g) of white fondant into a circle $\frac{1}{4}$ in (6 mm) thick and no larger than a dinner plate.

2 Slide your hand under the fondant, lift it up, and gently place it on top of the cakelet. Smooth it down and around the cake.

3 Cut away the excess fondant with a pastry wheel.

4 Place the cakelet in the refrigerator to chill for 30 minutes.

Decorate the ornament

1 Dust a clean, dry work surface with cornstarch. Roll out 2 oz (55 g) of green fondant until it's $\frac{1}{8}$ in (3 mm) thick. Cut a strip that's 1 in (2.5 cm) wide and 12 in (30.5 cm) long.

2 Brush some water on the back of the strip, then wrap it around the middle of the cakelet to adhere it, with the seam in the back.

3 Use a stitching tool to add some detail next to the top and bottom edges of the green strip.

4 Brush the back of the green button with water and adhere it to the middle of the green strip.

5 Dust a clean, dry work surface with cornstarch. Roll out the remainder of the green fondant into a sheet $\frac{1}{4}$ in (6 mm) thick. Use the 3-in (7.5-cm) circle cutter to cut out a circle.

6 Brush one side of the 3-in (7.5-cm) circle with water and adhere it to the top of the ornament where you will be attaching the hook.

7 Dust a clean, dry work surface with cornstarch. Roll out 1 oz (28 g) of white fondant into a circle $\frac{1}{2}$ in (1.25 cm) thick. Use a flower cutter to cut out a flower for the base of the hook. Brush with water and adhere it to the middle of the green circle on top of the ornament.

8 Brush the flower with a little water and adhere the base of the hook to it.

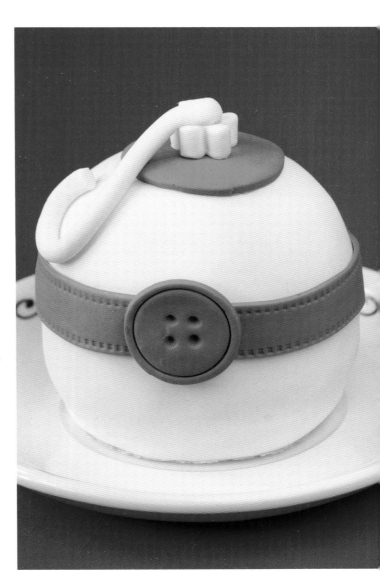

Party Time!

No matter how old we are, party hats bring out the kid in all of us. Whether you're looking for a birthday-appropriate cakelet for a 5-year-old or a 50-year-old, these festive hats are a slam-dunk. They're sure to make everyone smile and they're very easy to make, to boot. Try customizing them with the name of each party guest, or use flowers or spiraling stripes instead of dots.

Tools
The Necessities (pages 11–12)
6-cavity Wilton king-size muffin pan
$\frac{3}{4}$-in (1.8-cm) circle cutter
$\frac{1}{2}$-in (1.25-cm) circle cutter
Cake decorating tip #2A

Ingredients
**One 16-oz (455-g) box cake mix (any flavor)
   prepared, or batter for one 9-in (23-cm) cake**
**1 recipe Vanilla Frosting (page 17) or 1
   container store-bought frosting**
**1 lb (455 g) white fondant
   (see Resources, page 114)**
**Pink, blue, yellow, orange, and green gel food
   colorings**

Bake the cake
1   Preheat oven to 350°F (180°C). Spray each cavity of the king-size muffin pan to be used with non-stick spray (you will need one muffin cake for one cakelet). Fill each cavity being used three-quarters full with batter. Bake for 25 minutes, or until the top springs back when lightly pressed and a toothpick inserted into the center comes out clean.

2   Allow the cake to cool in the pan. If the cake rose above the pan, use a serrated knife to cut away the top of the cake to make it level (set the knife across the top of the pan so you

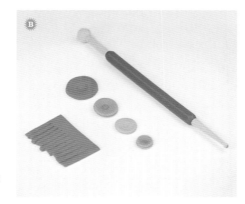

can use it as a guide). When completely cool, run a knife around the edge to loosen the sides. Invert the cake out of the pan and wrap in plastic wrap. Freeze for at least two hours until cold and firm.

Prepare to decorate
1   Divide 4 oz (115 g) of the white fondant into four equal portions. Use the gel food coloring to tint each one of the following colors: pink, blue, yellow, and green. (See tinting instructions on page 16.)

2   Use the orange gel food coloring to tint 3 oz (85 g) of the white fondant orange.

3   Remove the cake from the freezer and unwrap. Place it upside down on parchment.

4   Use a serrated knife to cut away the sides of the cake to make the shape of a party hat. Start each angled cut at the top of the cake and slice down. ✳

5   Using a tapered angled spatula, crumb coat the cakelet with Vanilla Frosting. Use enough frosting so that the spatula doesn't come into direct contact with the cake. This will keep you from dislodging too many crumbs.

Cover the cakelet
1   Dust a clean, dry work surface with cornstarch. Roll out 9 oz (255 g) of white fondant into a sheet $\frac{1}{4}$ in (6 mm) thick.

2   Wrap the fondant around the cake. Use scissors to cut away the excess fondant on top

Level *Easy/Intermediate*
Batter yields enough cake for *4 cakelets*
Fondant quantity listed is suitable to complete *1 cakelet*

of the cake. Use an X-Acto knife to cut away excess fondant along the side of the cake to make a smooth seam. Use the pastry wheel trim away excess fondant at the base.

Finishing touches

1 Dust a clean, dry work surface with cornstarch. Roll out 1 oz (28 g) of orange fondant into a strip 6 in (15 cm) long, 1 in (2.5 cm) wide, and $\frac{1}{8}$ in (3 mm) thick.

2 Use a knife to cut fringe along the bottom of the strip. **B**

3 Roll the fringed strip up and pinch the bottom end to form a tassel. Cut away any excess fondant. Adhere the tassel to the top of the party hat with a little water.

4 Roll out the blue, pink, yellow, and green fondant into sheets that are $\frac{1}{4}$ in (6 mm) thick. Cut out an assortment of circles using the small circle cutters and the #2A cake decorating tip (if the circles get stuck in the tip, use the end of a paintbrush to push them out). Use a variety of ball tools to create a depression in the middle of each circle. Adhere the circles to the party hat with a little water.

5 Roll out 2 oz (55 g) of orange fondant into a strip 10 in (25.5 cm) long, 1 in (2.5 cm) wide and $\frac{1}{8}$ in (3 mm) thick. Use a knife to cut fringe along the bottom of the strip.

6 Adhere the strip to the base of the hat with a little water. Line up the seam with the seam of the white fondant. Trim away any excess.

What's Love Got to Do with It?

Sure, Valentine's Day is great—when you're not single. For everyone out there flying solo and feeling bitter on this lovey-dovey holiday, this one's for you. Take out your hatred of an ex-from-hell by stabbing this voodoo doll with a fork, then eating its heart out. You'll get both dessert and catharsis with every bite.

Tools
9 x 6-in (23 x 15-cm) metal brownie pan
The Necessities (pages 11–12)
Voodoo Doll template (see Templates, page 115)
Cake decorating tips: #2A, #5, #10
Heart-shaped cutter
Ball tool or end of a paintbrush
Stitching tool (see Resources, page 114)
Toothpick

Ingredients
One 16-oz (455-g) box cake mix (any flavor) prepared, or batter for one 9-in (23-cm) cake
1 recipe Vanilla Frosting (page 17) or 1 container store-bought frosting
1 lb (455 g) black fondant (see Resources, page 114)
1 oz (28 g) red fondant (see Resources, page 114)
1 oz (28 g) white fondant (see Resources, page 114)

Bake the cake
1 Preheat oven to 350°F (180°C). Prepare the cake batter. Spray the brownie pan with non-stick spray.

2 Pour the batter into the pan, filling it three-quarters full. Smooth the top and bake for 20–30 minutes, or until the top springs back when lightly pressed and a toothpick inserted into the center comes out clean.

3 Place the pan on a wire rack to cool for about 10 minutes. If the cake rose above the pan, use a serrated knife to cut away the top of the cake to make it level (set the knife across the top of the pan so you can use it as a guide). Run a knife around the edge to loosen the sides. Invert the cake out of the pan onto a wire rack and allow to cool. When completely cool, wrap in plastic wrap and freeze for at least two hours until cold and firm.

Prepare to decorate
1 Remove the cake from the freezer and unwrap. Place the Voodoo Doll template on top of the cake and use a sharp knife to cut out the cake around it. Remove the template and use the knife to clean up any rough edges. ✺

2 Gently place the cakelet on a piece of parchment. Using a tapered angled spatula, crumb coat the cakelet with Vanilla Frosting starting around the sides of the cake and finishing on the top. Use enough frosting so that the spatula doesn't come into direct contact with the cake. This will keep you from dislodging too many crumbs. (If you find that the cake has thawed and is difficult to coat, rewrap and place in the refrigerator or freezer until it's firm again.)

Level *Intermediate*
Batter yields enough cake for *1 cakelet*
Fondant quantity listed is suitable to complete *1 cakelet*

Cover the cakelet

1 Dust a clean, dry work surface with cornstarch. Roll out the black fondant into a sheet $\frac{1}{4}$ in (6 mm) thick and large enough to cover the cakelet.

2 Slide your hands underneath the fondant using open palms so as not to poke a hole in the fondant. Pick it up and lay it over the cakelet. Smooth the top of it first, using an open palm. Then smooth the fondant down over the sides. When smoothing around the arms and in between the legs, work quickly but gently so as not to tear the fondant.

3 Use a pastry wheel to cut away excess fondant around the bottom of the cakelet. Use an X-Acto knife to remove excess fondant underneath the arms and between the legs.

Assemble

Feet and Hands: Using your hands, roll a piece of the white fondant into two thin 4-in (10-cm) strips. Cut the two strips in half. Cross the white fondant strips to form an "X." Brush the tops of the feet with a bit of water and lay the Xs on top. Repeat process for the hands.

Eyes: Roll out a piece of red fondant into a sheet $\frac{1}{8}$ in (3 mm) thick. Repeat with a piece of white fondant. Use a #2A tip to cut out one circle from each piece. Roll out a piece of black fondant until it's $\frac{1}{8}$ in (3 mm) thick and use #5 tip to cut out a circle for the inner part of one eye. Use a #10 tip for the pupil of the other eye. ⑧ Brush the center of each eye with a bit of water and set the black circles on top. Adhere the eyes to the face with a bit of water.

Mouth: Use your hands to roll out a piece of white fondant into a skinny strip. Use a bit of water to adhere it to the face in a jagged manner. Cut several small strips of white fondant and adhere them across the mouth so it looks poorly sewn.

Heart: Roll out a piece of red fondant until it's $\frac{1}{8}$ in (3 mm) thick. Use a heart-shaped cutter to cut out a heart. Adhere to the chest of the doll with a bit of water.

Border: Use a stitching tool to add a stitched effect around the top edge of the cakelet.

Arrow: Roll out a small piece of white fondant into a sheet $\frac{1}{8}$ in (3 mm) thick. Use an X-Acto knife to cut out three small parallelograms. Cut slits in them to form the arrow's feathers. Adhere the feathers to the end of the arrow with a dab of water. Insert the arrow into the heart.

I ♥ U

Initials carved in a tree—a public declaration of undying love that will last for generations. (To this day, there is a tree in my parents' backyard where I carved the initials of a boy I loved way back in 4th grade.) This cakelet is a classic symbol of romance and a sweet way to celebrate the one you love.

Tools

The Necessities (pages 11–12)
6-cavity Wilton king-size muffin pan
Flower Pot template (see Templates, page 115)
2½-in (6.25-cm) circle cutter
2-in (5-cm) circle cutter
Toothpick
Heart-shaped cutter
Small flower blossom cutter

Ingredients

One 16-oz (455-g) box cake mix (any flavor)
  prepared, or batter for one 9-in (23-cm) cake
1 recipe Vanilla Frosting (page 17) or
  1 container store-bought frosting
1 lb (455 g) chocolate or brown fondant
  (see Resources, page 114)
8 oz (225 g) white fondant
  (see Resources, page 114)
Pink gel food coloring
Green gel food coloring

Bake the cake

1 Preheat oven to 350°F (180°C). Spray each cavity of the king-size muffin pan to be used with non-stick spray (you will need one muffin cake for one cakelet). Fill each cavity being used three-quarters full with batter. Bake for 25 minutes, or until the top springs back when lightly pressed and a toothpick inserted into the center comes out clean.

2 Allow the cake to cool in the pan. If the cake rose above the pan, use a serrated knife to cut away the top of the cake to make it level (set the knife across the top of the pan so you can use it as a guide). When completely cool,

Level *Easy/Intermediate*
Batter yields enough cake for *4 cakelets*
Fondant quantity listed is suitable to complete *1 cakelet*

run a knife around the edges to loosen the sides. Invert the cake out of the pan and wrap in plastic wrap. Freeze for at least two hours until cold and firm.

Prepare to decorate

1 Tint 2 oz (55 g) of white fondant with the pink gel color, and 2 oz (55 g) with the green gel color. Knead together 4 oz (115 g) of the white fondant with a pinch of chocolate fondant to make it off-white in color. Wrap each tinted fondant separately in plastic wrap until ready to use.

2 Remove the king-size muffin cake from the freezer and unwrap. Place upside down (wide-end down) on a piece of parchment.

3 Using a tapered angled spatula, crumb coat the cakelets with Vanilla Frosting starting at the sides and finishing at the top. Use enough frosting so that the spatula doesn't come into direct contact with the cake. This will keep you from dislodging too many crumbs.

Cover the cakelet

1 Dust a clean, dry work surface with cornstarch. Roll out the off-white fondant into a sheet $\frac{1}{8}$ in (3 mm) thick. Use the circle cutters to cut out a $2\frac{1}{2}$-in (6.25-cm) circle and a 2-in (5-cm) circle.

2 Place the larger circle on top of the tree stump and use the fondant marking tool to create the look of growth rings.

3 Use the toothpick to carve initials or names

into the smaller circle and adhere it to the side of the tree stump.

4 Roll out the chocolate fondant into a sheet $\frac{1}{4}$ in (6 mm) thick and approximately the size of the Flower Pot template. Place the Flower

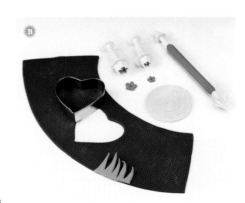

Pot template on top and use a pastry wheel to cut out the shape, using the template as a guide. Use the heart cutter to cut a heart out of the middle.

5 Wrap the piece of chocolate fondant neatly around the cakelet, placing the cut-out heart over the off-white fondant with the names carved into it. Use the pastry wheel to cut away excess fondant around the base of the cake.

Finishing touches

1 Use the small ball tool to indent vertical lines around the bark of the stump. Vary the lines and don't make them too straight, so they look realistic.

2 Roll out the green fondant into a sheet $\frac{1}{8}$ in (3 mm) thick. Use a pastry cutter or an X-Acto knife to cut out stalks of grass in various widths and lengths.

3 Adhere the grass around the base of the stump using water and small paintbrush. Try curling the grass spears for a whimsical look.

4 Roll out the pink fondant into a sheet $\frac{1}{8}$ in (3 mm) thick. Use the small blossom cutter to cut out 20–30 pink flowers.

5 Adhere the flowers in clusters around the base of the stump using water and a small paint brush.

6 Press the flower veiner tool into the center of each blossom to add a little detail.

How Does Your Garden Grow?

Level *Intermediate*
Batter yields enough cake for *4 cakelets*
Fondant quantity listed is suitable to complete *1 cakelet*

Flowers on a cake are nothing new, but a cake shaped like a barrel of flowers is something you don't see every day. This pretty cakelet combines things we always turn to for special occasions into a form that's unexpected and exciting. This design is versatile and customizable. It even works beautifully as a get-well or sympathy gift.

Tools
6-cavity Wilton king-size muffin pan
The Necessities (pages 11–12)
Flower Pot template (see Templates, page 115)
Small and medium flower cutters
Flower veiner tool

Ingredients
One 16-oz (455-g) box cake mix (any flavor) prepared, or batter for one 9-in (23-cm) cake
1 recipe Vanilla Frosting (page 17) or 1 container store-bought frosting
8 oz (225 g) chocolate fondant or brown colored fondant (see Resources, page 114)
1 lb (455 g) white fondant (see Resources, page 114)
Pink, blue, yellow, and green gel food colorings
Several pieces of uncooked spaghetti

Bake the cake
1 Preheat oven to 350°F (180°C). Spray each of the king-size muffin pan cavities to be used with a non-stick spray (you will need one muffin cake for one cakelet). Fill each of the king-sized muffin cavities being used three-quarters full with batter. Bake for 25 minutes, or until the top springs back when lightly pressed and a toothpick inserted into the center comes out clean.

2 Allow the cake to cool for a few minutes in the pan. If the cake rose above the pan, use a serrated knife to cut away the top to make it level (set the knife across the top of the pan so you can use it as a guide). Run a knife around the edge to loosen the sides. Invert the cake out of the pan and place on a wire rack to finish cooling. ✸ When completely cool, wrap in plastic wrap and freeze for at least two hours until cold and firm.

Prepare to decorate
Divide 8 oz (225 g) of white fondant into quarters. Color each portion in the shades desired for the flowers and leaves (see tinting instructions on page 16). Wrap each color separately in plastic wrap until ready to use.

Cover the cake
1 Place the king-sized muffin cake upside down on a square of parchment paper, so the narrow end of the cake is up.

2 Using a tapered angled spatula, apply a smooth crumb coat of Vanilla Frosting on the sides of the cake (but not the top). Use enough frosting so that the spatula doesn't come into direct contact with the cake. This will keep you from dislodging too many crumbs.

3 Mix together 7 oz (200 g) of white fondant with 1 oz (28 g) chocolate or brown colored fondant. Dust a clean, dry work surface with cornstarch. Roll out the off-white fondant into a 4½-in (11.25-cm) by 11-in (28-cm) rectangle that's ¼ in (6 mm) thick. Place the Flower Pot template on top and use a pastry wheel to cut out the shape, using the template as a guide.

4 Use an X-Acto knife to cut "staves" for what will become the half barrel flower container. Cut the ends at odd angles to give them character. Use the fondant marking tool to create the impression of wood grain. ✸

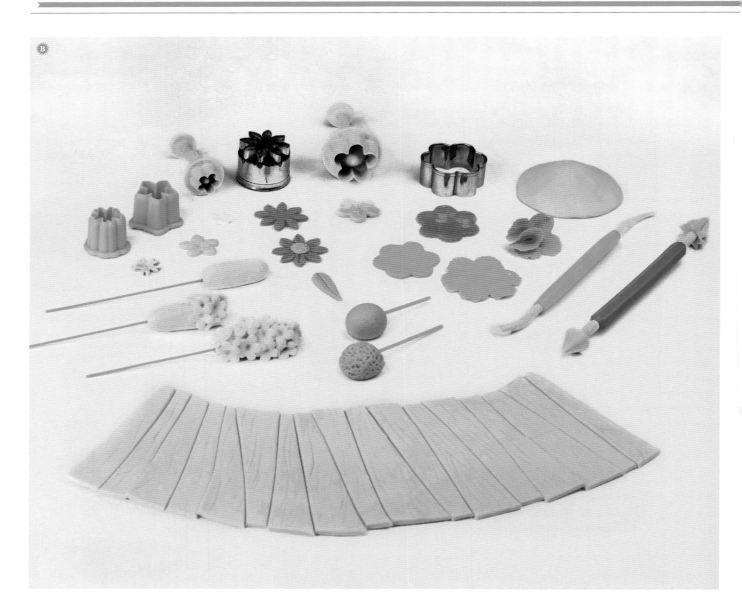

5 Gently wrap the pieces around the cake so that the seams touch. Cut away any excess fondant around the bottom of the cake.

6 Roll out 3 oz (85 g) of chocolate or brown colored fondant into two strips 10 in (25.5 cm) long, 1 in (2.5 cm) wide, and $\frac{1}{8}$ in (3 mm) thick. Using a little water, adhere the strips around the barrel, forming the hoops, with the seams in the back. Trim away the excess at the seam. Refrigerate for one hour.

Assemble

1 Remove the cakelet from the refrigerator and place it right side up on a fresh piece of parchment paper.

2 Using a tapered angled spatula, apply a smooth crumb coat of Vanilla Frosting to the top of the cakelet.

3 Roll out the green fondant until it is $\frac{1}{8}$ in (3 mm) thick. Cut a circle roughly the same size as the opening of the barrel and lay it over the mouth, smoothing it down. Cut away any excess fondant with an X-Acto knife.

4 Dust a clean, dry work surface with cornstarch. Roll out 1 oz (28 g) of white fondant into a 2-in (5-cm) ball. Flatten the bottom of the ball and use a little water to adhere it to the green circle.

Make and adhere the flowers

1 Roll a gumball-sized piece of white fondant into a log. Dip an end of raw spaghetti in water and insert it into the log. Using a small flower

cutter, cut out approximately twenty small flowers and adhere them to the fondant log in close formation. Make two or three of these, and insert them into the top of the cakelet.

2 Using your hands, roll a gumball-sized piece of green fondant. Dip an end of raw spaghetti in water and insert it into the ball. Texture the ball with a toothpick. Make two or three of these, and insert them into the top of the cakelet.

3 Roll out the lightest shade of fondant until it's $\frac{1}{8}$ in (3 mm) thick. Using the small flower cutter, cut out 15–20 flowers.

4 Brush the top of the cakelet with water. Arrange the flowers around the opening of the barrel. Using the flower veining tool, press the tip into each flower, attaching it to the surface.

5 Repeat steps 4 and 5 using different shades of fondant and different sized flower cutters until the top of the cakelet is covered.

Tip: Using randomly arranged flowers in a variety of sizes, colors, and shapes makes for a more natural-looking arrangement.

Finishing touches

Dress up your cakelet by adding green fondant leaves. You might also add a monogram plate to the front of the container, or pipe a dot of royal icing into the center of each blossom for added detail.

Trick or Treat!

The best part about carving pumpkins is making them as scary or goofy as your carving skills allow. Trouble is, there's no way around creating a big goopy mess in the process. My solution? Make a jack-o'-lantern cakelet instead. Even kids can make them with ease. They're the perfect dessert for Halloween parties and ideal as a table decoration—and you can eat it when the party's over.

Tools
6-cavity Wilton mini ball pan
The Necessities (pages 11–12)
Fondant smoother

Ingredients
One 16-oz (455 g) box cake mix (any flavor) prepared, or batter for one 9-in (23-cm) cake
1 recipe Vanilla Frosting (page 17) or 1 container store-bought frosting
5 oz (145 g) orange fondant (see Resources, page 114)
1 oz (28 g) black fondant (see Resources, page 114)
2 oz (55 g) green fondant (see Resources, page 114)
1 wooden skewer or drinking straw

Bake the cakes
1 Preheat oven to 350°F (180°C). Spray each of the mini ball cavities to be used with non-stick spray (you will need two mini ball cakes for one cakelet). Fill each cavity being used three-quarters full with batter. Bake for 10–12 minutes, or until the tops spring back when lightly pressed and a toothpick inserted into the center comes out clean.

2 Allow the cakes to cool for a few minutes in the pan. If the cakes are domed, use a serrated knife to trim the cakes until they are level (use the top of the pan as your guide). Run a knife around the edges to loosen the sides. Invert the cakes out of the pan onto a wire rack to finish cooling. When completely cool, wrap each in plastic wrap and freeze for at least two hours until cold and firm.

Prepare the cakelet
1 Remove two cakes from the freezer and unwrap. Place each cake flat side down on a piece of parchment and cut away any hard edges.

2 Using a tapered angled spatula, apply a layer of Vanilla Frosting to the bottom of one of the ball cakes. Adhere the bottom of another cake to it to form a sphere. ⚙

3 Cut away any rough edges where the two halves meet to make for a smooth seam. Cut out a wedge from the sphere so that the cakelet can sit flat.

4 Crumb coat the sphere with Vanilla Frosting. Use enough frosting so that the spatula doesn't come into direct contact with the cake. This will keep you from dislodging too many crumbs.

Cover the cakelet
1 Dust a clean, dry work surface with

cornstarch. Roll out about 5 oz (145 g) of orange fondant into a circle $\frac{1}{4}$ in (6 mm) thick and no larger than a dinner plate.

2 Slide your hand under the fondant, lift it up, and gently place it on top of a cakelet. Smooth it down and around the cake.

3 Cut away excess fondant with a pastry

Level *Easy*
Batter yields enough cake for *3 cakelets*
Fondant quantity listed is suitable to complete *1 cakelet*

wheel. Use a medium ball tool to press indented lines from top to bottom, giving the pumpkin realistic ridges. Make sure the lines intersect at the top of the pumpkin. Use the ball tool to press a conical mark where the lines intersect. This is where stem will be placed.

4 Place in the refrigerator to chill for 30 minutes.

Finishing touches

1 Remove the fondant-covered cakelet from the refrigerator.

2 Dust a clean, dry work surface with cornstarch. Roll out half of the green fondant into a log $1\frac{1}{4}$ in (3.1 cm) long and $\frac{1}{2}$ in (1.25 cm) thick. Use a fondant scoring tool to add texture to the stem.

3 To create the vines. Roll out a thin log of fondant approximately 6 in (15 cm) long. To make the log an even width, use a fondant smoother to roll the fondant back and forth.

4 Wrap the green fondant roll around a skewer or drinking straw to create a corkscrew.

5 Leave the wrapped vine in place for 10 minutes.

6 Slide the skewer or drinking straw out from within the vine spiral, and cut the vine in half.

7 Use water to adhere one end of a curly vine to the top of the pumpkin.

8 Repeat to adhere the second vine.

9 Brush a little water onto the top of the pumpkin and adhere the green stem. Slightly bend the stem for a realistic look.

10 Dust a clean, dry work surface with cornstarch. Roll out the black fondant into a sheet $\frac{1}{4}$ in (6 mm) thick. Cut out shapes for the eyes, nose, and mouth of the jack-o'-lantern. Brush a little water onto the front of the pumpkin and adhere the shapes.

Boo!

Why does a ghost have to be spooky? How about a girly ghost? Or a funky ghost? Or a ghost that wears a costume? This easy design offers the biggest range of decorating possibilities. You can make it ultra simple with just black eyes and a black mouth or go all out and give it a wardrobe of accessories. If making optional arms, be sure to form them a day in advance to allow for drying time.

Tools

12-cavity muffin pan
Cupcake liners or nonstick spray
The Necessities (pages 11–12)
Cake decorating tip #12

Ingredients

One 16-oz (455-g) box cake mix (any flavor) prepared, or batter for one 9-in (23-cm) cake
1 recipe Vanilla Frosting (page 17) or 1 container store-bought frosting
8 oz (225 g) white fondant, or 10 oz (285 g) if creating optional arms (see Resources, page 114)
4 oz (115 g) black fondant
1 recipe Royal Icing—optional (page 17)
1 piece of uncooked spaghetti—optional

Prepare the arms—optional (1–2 days prior to decorating)

1 If including arms on your ghost, dust a clean, dry work surface with cornstarch. Roll out 2 oz (55 g) of white fondant into a log $\frac{3}{4}$ in (1.8 cm) thick and 5 in (12.5 cm) long. Cut the log in half to create two arms.

2 Gently flatten one end of each arm and use a small ball tool to push in part of the flattened area to create the impression of thumbs.

3 If you wish the arms to hold a pose, dip the ends of pieces of uncooked spaghetti into water, and then insert one into the shoulder end of each arm. Allow the fondant arms to dry for 1–2 days before attaching them to the ghosts.

Bake the cupcakes

1 Preheat oven to 350°F (180°C). Line the muffin tin cavities to be used with cupcake liners or spray with nonstick spray (you will need at least two cupcakes for one cakelet—use three for a taller ghost).

2 Spoon the batter into the muffin cups, filling each three-quarters full. Bake for approximately 20 minutes, or until the tops spring back when lightly pressed and a toothpick inserted into the centers comes out clean.

3 Place the pan on a wire rack to cool. If the cupcakes rose above the tops of the cups, use a serrated knife to make them level (set the knife across the top of the pan so you can use it as a guide). When completely cool, wrap in plastic wrap and freeze for at least two hours until cold and firm.

Prepare the cakelet

1 If you used cupcake liners, peel away and discard. ✺

2 Coat the top of one cupcake in Vanilla Frosting and set another cupcake on top. If you want a taller ghost, stack a third cupcake on top, using more frosting to adhere it. Place the cakelet on a piece of parchment.

3 Using a tapered angled spatula, crumb coat the cakelet with Vanilla Frosting, starting around the sides and finishing at the top. Use enough frosting so that the spatula doesn't come into direct contact with the cake. This will keep you from dislodging too many crumbs.

Level **Easy**
Batter yields enough cake for **6 cakelets**
Fondant quantity listed is suitable to complete **1 cakelet**

Covering the cakelet

1 Dust a clean, dry work surface with cornstarch. Roll out 8 oz (225 g) of white fondant into a circle $\frac{1}{4}$ in (6 mm) thick and no larger than a salad plate.

2 Slide your hand under the fondant, lift it up, and gently place it on top of the cakelet. Do not smooth it down yet; instead, allow the fondant to naturally drape, making for a more realistic looking sheet. Once it looks the way you like, gently smooth the top down and smooth around the sides of the cake to adhere it.

3 Cut away excess fondant with a pastry wheel.

4 Place in the refrigerator to chill for 30 minutes.

Finishing touches

The ghost is a blank slate. You can dress it up as silly or as ghoulish as you like. Try giving it luscious lips and eyelashes, glasses or a hat, a funny hair style, mustache, or fashion accessories like earrings and a purse.

Eyes: Roll out 1 oz (28 g) of black fondant and use cake decorating tip #12 to cut out circles for eyes. Adhere with a dab of water.

Mouth: Use a black fondant oval adhered with a dab of water, or tint some of the royal icing red and pipe a mouth onto the ghost.

Hair (optional): Tint some royal icing your preferred color. Use it to fill a piping bag fitted with the grass tip. Pipe hair onto the ghost.

Pomp and Circumstance

Graduations are no small feat. The culmination of years of hard work and perseverance, they deserve to be celebrated with as much fanfare as you can muster—and a cakelet! This is one graduation cap I guarantee won't get thrown into the air, and it's so cute, it'll likely be as well-photographed as the graduates themselves. The design is perfect for customizing with school colors, names, and the graduating year, and it also works great for school reunions.

Tools
The Necessities (pages 11–12)
6-cavity Wilton king-size muffin pan
Toothpick
Ruler
Flower Pot template
  (see Templates, page 115)
Graduation Band template
  (see Templates, page 115)
Fondant smoother

Ingredients
One 16-oz (455-g) box cake mix (any flavor)
  prepared, or batter for one 9-in (23-cm) cake
1 recipe Vanilla Frosting (page 17) or 1
  container store-bought frosting
10 oz (285 g) white fondant
  (see Resources, page 17)
Green gel food coloring (or color of your
  choice)
1 recipe Royal Icing (page 17)
Gold luster dust
1 teaspoon vodka

Create the top (three days prior to decorating)
1 Color the fondant with the green gel food coloring. Wrap all but 2 oz (55 g) in plastic and place in an airtight container.

2 Dust a clean, dry work surface with cornstarch. Roll out the 2 oz (55 g) of green fondant into an 4-in (10-cm) square sheet $\frac{1}{8}$ in (3 mm) thick for the top of the cap. Use the flower veiner to add radial creases in the middle of the square. Place on a piece of parchment paper and set aside to dry out for three days at room temperature out of direct sunlight (to keep the color from fading).

Bake the cake
1 Preheat oven to 350°F (180°C). Spray each of the king-size muffin pan cavities to be used with a non-stick spray (you will need one muffin cake for one cakelet). Fill each cavity being used three-quarters full with batter. Bake for 25 minutes, or until the top springs back when lightly pressed and a toothpick inserted into the center comes out clean.

2 Allow the cake to cool for a few minutes in the pan. If the cake rose above the pan, use a serrated knife to cut away the top to make it level (set the knife across the top of the pan so you can use it as a guide). Run a knife around the edges to loosen the sides. Invert the cake out of the pan and place on a wire rack to finish cooling. When completely cool, wrap the cake in plastic wrap and freeze for at least two hours until cold and firm.

Prepare to decorate
1 Place the cake upside down onto a square of parchment paper so the narrow end of the cake is up.

2 Using a tapered angled spatula, apply a smooth crumb coat of Vanilla Frosting on the cake. Use enough frosting so that the spatula doesn't come into direct contact with the cake. This will keep you from dislodging too many crumbs.

3 Dust a clean, dry work surface with cornstarch. Roll out 6 oz (200 g) of green fondant into a 4½-in (11.25-cm) by 11-in (28-cm) rectangle that's ¼ in (6 mm) thick.

Level *Easy/Intermediate*
Batter yields enough cake for *4 cakelets*
Fondant quantity listed is suitable to complete *1 cakelet*

Place the Flower Pot template on top and use a pastry wheel to cut the fondant, using the template as a guide.

4 Gently pick up the fondant and wrap it around the cake so that the seams touch. Cut away any excess fondant around the bottom of the cake with a pastry wheel.

5 Roll out some of the remaining green fondant into a strip 10 in (25.5 cm) long by 1 in (2.5 cm) wide and $\frac{1}{4}$ in (6 mm) thick. Place the Graduation Band template on top and use the pastry wheel to cut the fondant, using the template as a guide.

6 Lightly brush water across the bottom of the cakelet and place the strip place around it to form the decorated edge. Cut away any excess fondant with scissors. Make sure that the seams line up.

7 Dab a little frosting on the top of the cakelet. Adhere the dried green square. Refrigerate for one hour.

Make the tassel

1 Dust a clean, dry work surface with cornstarch. Roll out a thin, 3 in (7.5 cm) long log of green fondant. Place the fondant smoother on top of the log and roll it back and forth to get an evenly formed roll.

2 Flatten one end of the log. Use an X-Acto knife to cut multiple slits to make the end of the tassel.

3 Lightly brush the top of the cap with water and adhere the tassel.

4 Roll out a small piece of green fondant. Cut it into a rectangle and adhere it around the end of the log with a dab of water. This forms a cuff above where the fringed "skirt" begins.

5 Roll a small ball of green fondant. Lightly brush the area where the tassel is attached to the cap and adhere the ball.

6 In a small bowl, mix a small amount of gold luster dust with vodka (it should be the consistency of thick gravy).

7 Brush the mixture onto the cuff and tassel, and the top of the decorative border around the base of the graduation cap.

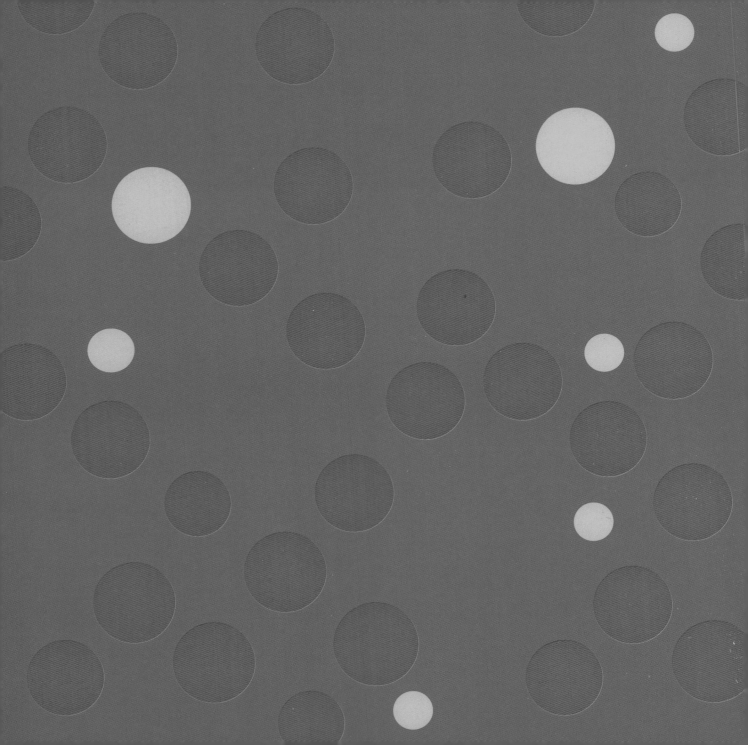

Chapter 8

Offbeat and Edgy

The Joke's on You!

Level *Easy/Intermediate*
Batter yields enough cake for *4 cakelets*
Fondant quantity listed is suitable to complete *1 cakelet*

I live for a good prank—just ask my neighbors. Throughout the years these good sports have fallen victim to many of my ridiculous stunts. This collection of mini cakes is a celebration of those classic pranks we all know and love. Try your favorite, or make all three!

Tools

9 x 13-in (23 x 33-cm) cake pan
The Necessities (pages 11–12)
2 fondant smoothers
Mustache template—optional (see Templates, page 115)
Small circle cutter
Small flower cutter
Texture sponge—optional

Ingredients

One 16-oz (455-g) box cake mix (any flavor) prepared, or batter for one 9-in (23-cm) cake
1 recipe Vanilla Frosting (page 17) or 1 container store-bought frosting
For the mustache cakelet: 12 oz (340 g) white fondant, 6 oz (170 g) black fondant, and 1 oz (28 g) red fondant (see Resources, page 114)
For the doggy poo cakelet: 12 oz (340 g) white fondant, 4 oz (115 g) black fondant, and 4 oz (115 g) chocolate or brown fondant (see Resources, page 114)
For the fake arrow through the head cakelet: 1 lb (455 g) white fondant, 5 oz (140 g) black fondant, and 2 oz (55 g) red fondant (see Resources, page 114)

Prepare the fondant centerpiece (one day prior to decorating)

Mustache

1 Dust a clean, dry work surface with cornstarch. Roll out a small handful of black fondant until it is $\frac{1}{4}$ in (6 mm) thick and 3 in (7.5 cm) long.

2 Place mustache template on top of the fondant and use an X-Acto knife to cut out the mustache shape  and place on parchment paper to dry.

Doggy poo

1 Dust a clean, dry work surface with cornstarch. Roll out a small handful of chocolate or brown fondant into a log approximately 7 in (17.5 cm) long and $\frac{3}{4}$ in (1.8 cm) thick.

2 Use the texture sponge to roughen the surface of the log.

3 Twist the textured log into a swirl and place on parchment paper to dry.

Challenge: Try sculpting a fly out of fondant and place on the swirl for a bigger gross-out effect.

Fake arrow through the head
1 Dust a clean, dry work surface with cornstarch. Take a small handful of white fondant and mix it with a pinch of black fondant to make a uniform gray tone. Roll it into a thin log approximately $3\frac{1}{2}$ in (9 cm) long. Use a fondant smoother to roll it into an arrow shaft with a half-circle bend in the middle (use the outside of a small circle cutter to create the arc).

2 Roll out a small piece of black fondant until $\frac{1}{4}$ in (6 mm) thick. Use an X-Acto knife to cut out a small triangle for the arrowhead. Adhere it to one end of the arrow with a dab of water.

3 Roll out a small piece of black fondant until $\frac{1}{4}$ in (6 mm) thick. Use an X-Acto knife to cut out three small parallelograms.

4 Use the knife to cut slits in the parallelograms to make the feathers of the arrow. With a dab of water, adhere the feathers to the end of the arrow.

5 Set the arrow aside on parchment paper to dry.

Bake the cake
1 Preheat oven to 350°F (180°C). Prepare the cake batter. Spray the cake pan with non-stick spray.

2 Pour the batter into the pan, filling it three-quarters full. Smooth the top and bake for 30–40 minutes, or until the top springs back when lightly pressed and a toothpick inserted into the center comes out clean.

3 Place pan on a wire rack to cool for about 10 minutes. If the cake rose above the pan, use a serrated knife to cut away the top of the cake to make it level (set the knife across the top of the pan so you can use it as a guide). Run a knife around the edge to loosen the sides. Invert the cake out of the pan onto a wire rack and allow to finish cooling. When completely cool, wrap in plastic wrap and freeze for at least two hours until cold and firm.

Covering the cakelet
1 Remove the cake from the freezer and unwrap. Use a serrated knife to cut it into

3-in (7.5-cm) squares (you will need two squares for one cakelet). Place a square on a piece of parchment.

2 Using a tapered angled spatula, apply a smooth layer of Vanilla Frosting on top of the square. Set another cake square on top of the frosted square. **B**

3 Using a tapered angled spatula, crumb coat the cakelet with Vanilla Frosting starting at the sides and finishing at the top. Use enough frosting so that the spatula doesn't come into direct contact with the cake. This will keep you from dislodging too many crumbs.

4 Dust a clean, dry work surface with cornstarch. Roll out 12 oz (340 g) of white fondant until it is $\frac{1}{4}$ in (6 mm) thick.

5 Slide your hand under the fondant, lift it up, and gently place it on top of the cakelet and smooth it down and around the cake. Use two fondant smoothers to smooth the top and sides of the cakes. Cut away excess fondant with a pastry wheel.

6 Place the cakelet in the refrigerator to chill for 30 minutes.

Assembly
1 Dust a clean, dry work surface with cornstarch. Roll out 4 oz (115 g) of black fondant until it is $\frac{1}{4}$ in (6 mm) thick and 12 in (30.5 cm) long. Cut out a strip $\frac{1}{2}$ in (1.25 cm) wide to make the bottom border of the cakelet.

2 Lightly brush water along the base of the cakelet and adhere the strip.

3 Lightly brush the top of the cakelet with water and adhere the "prank" on top. Add a dab or two of Vanilla Frosting behind the centerpieces for support, if necessary.

Finishing touches

Mustache

1 Dust a clean, dry work surface with cornstarch. Roll out 1 oz (28 g) of black fondant until it is $\frac{1}{8}$ in (3 mm) thick.

2 Use the small flower cutter to cut out twelve flowers.

3 Use a small ball tool to make an impression on each petal of the black flowers.

4 Use a dab of water to adhere them to the cake, three to a side.

5 Roll out twelve small pearls of red fondant. Pinch them to flatten, and adhere them to the centers of the black flowers with a dab of water.

Doggy poo

1 Dust a clean, dry work surface with cornstarch.

2 Roll out 4 oz (115 g) of chocolate or brown fondant until it is $\frac{1}{8}$ in (3 mm) thick, 1 in (2.5 cm) wide, and 12 in (30.5 cm) long.

3 Cut one long edge into a wavy shape with an X-Acto knife.

4 Lightly brush the area above the black strip with water, and adhere the wavy brown strip with the seam positioned on the same side as the seam of the bottom border.

Fake arrow through the head

1 Dust a clean, dry work surface with cornstarch.

2 Roll out 2 oz (55 g) of red fondant until it is $\frac{1}{8}$ in (3 mm) thick.

3 Roll out 2 oz (55 g) of white fondant until it is $\frac{1}{8}$ in (3 mm) thick.

4 Using a set of small circle cutters, cut out four sets of four circles in graduating sizes,

beginning with a set of four very small white circles, then a set of four slightly larger red circles, then a set of four slightly larger white circles, and ending with the largest set of four red circles.

5 Arrange these into four stacks of alternating red and white circles that resemble bulls-eyes when viewed head-on.

6 Adhere the layers of the stacks together with dabs of water.

7 Adhere the assembled stacks to the center of each vertical face of the cakelet with a little water.

Those Were the Days

An old-fashioned radio can remind us of simpler times—when you didn't need tech support to listen to some tunes. This charming cakelet is one everyone can appreciate.

Tools
9 x 5-in (23 x 12.5-cm) loaf pan
The Necessities (pages 11–12)
2 fondant smoothers
Small ball tool
1-in (2.5-cm) circle cutter
¾-in (1.8-cm) circle cutter
Oval cutter
Scoring tool
Toothpick
Fine-tipped paint brush

Ingredients
One 16-oz (455-g) box cake mix (any flavor)
  prepared, or batter for one 9-in (23-cm) cake
1 recipe Vanilla Frosting (page 17) or
  1 container store-bought frosting
9 oz (255 g) white fondant
  (see Resources, page 114)
4 oz (115 g) black fondant
  (see Resources, page 114)
3 oz (85 g) red fondant
  (see Resources, page 114)
Blue or teal gel food coloring
Black petal dust
2 tablespoons vodka

Bake the cake
1 Preheat oven to 350°F (180°C). Prepare the cake batter. Spray the loaf pan with non-stick spray.

2 Pour the batter into the pan, filling it three-quarters full. Smooth the top and bake for 25 minutes, or until the top springs back when lightly pressed and a toothpick inserted into the center comes out clean.

3 Place pan on a wire rack to cool for about 10 minutes. Run a knife around the edge of the pan to loosen the sides. Invert the cake out of the pan onto a wire rack and allow to finish cooling. When completely cool, wrap in plastic wrap and freeze for at least two hours until cold and firm.

Prepare to decorate
1 Use the blue or teal gel color to tint 8 oz (225 g) of the white fondant the desired color. Wrap the fondant in plastic wrap until ready to use.

2 Remove cake from the freezer and unwrap. Cut cake into a rectangle 5 in (12.5 cm) long, 3 in (7.5 cm) high and 3 in (7.5 cm) wide.

3 Starting at the top left corner of the cake, cut a gradual slope into the top of the cake, so that the left side of the cake is 3 in (7.5 cm)

high and the right side is 2 in (5 cm) high. Use your fingers to rub away the sharp edges.

4 Once the cake is shaped, slice it into two horizontal layers,  and add a layer of Vanilla Frosting between the two pieces.

5 Place cakelet on a piece of parchment. Using a tapered angled spatula, crumb coat the cakelet with Vanilla Frosting, starting at the sides and finishing at the top. Use enough frosting so that the spatula doesn't come into direct contact with the cake. This will keep you from dislodging too many crumbs.

Cover the cakelet
1 Dust a clean, dry work surface with cornstarch. Roll out the blue fondant into a sheet ¼ in (6 mm) thick.

2 Slide your hand under the fondant, lift up, and gently lay it onto the cakelet. Use an open palm to smooth the top of the cakelet first, then smooth down the sides.

3 Cut away excess fondant around the base with a pastry wheel.

Level *Intermediate*
Batter yields enough cake for *1 cakelet*
Fondant quantity listed is suitable to complete *1 cakelet*

4 Use the small ball tool to press an indented border around the front and back of the cakelet.

5 Use the two fondant smoothers to smooth the adjacent sides of the cake to create smooth edges.

6 Cut away excess fondant with a pastry wheel.

Finishing touches
Display
1 Dust a clean, dry work surface with cornstarch. Roll out 4 oz (115 g) of white fondant into a sheet $\frac{1}{8}$ in (3 mm) thick. Cut out a rectangle approximately $1\frac{3}{4}$ in (4.3 cm) long and $\frac{3}{4}$ in (2 cm) high. Starting at the top left corner of the rectangle, use the pastry wheel to give a gradual slope to the top, so that the left side is $\frac{3}{4}$ in (2 cm) high and the right side is $\frac{1}{2}$ in (1.25 cm) high. 🅑

2 On the front of the cakelet, use the small ball tool to gently make an indentation the same shape and size as the piece of white fondant.

3 Lightly brush the area with water and adhere the piece of white fondant to the cake.

4 Roll out a small piece of black fondant into a strip $1\frac{3}{4}$ in (4.3 cm) long, $\frac{1}{8}$ in (3 mm) high and $\frac{1}{4}$ in (6 mm) thick. Adhere to the bottom of the white fondant with a little water.

5 Roll out the red fondant until it's $\frac{1}{4}$-in (6 mm) thick and cut out a very small strip. Adhere to the white fondant with a little water to create the dial.

Speaker
1 Dust a clean, dry work surface with cornstarch. Roll out 1 oz (28 g) of black fondant out until it's $\frac{1}{4}$ in (6 mm) thick. Use the oval cutter to cut out an oval shape.

2 Use the pastry wheel to lightly indent a border around the surface of the oval. Use the scoring tool to indent multiple diagonal lines.

3 Use a little water to adhere the speaker on an angle to the front left side of cakelet.

Knobs and antenna
1 Dust a clean, dry work surface with cornstarch. Roll out 4 oz (115 g) of black fondant into a sheet $\frac{3}{4}$ in (1.8 cm) thick. Cut one 1-in (2.5-cm) circle and one $\frac{3}{4}$-in (1.8-cm) circle using the circle cutters to make the knobs.

2 Use a scoring tool or knife to create vertical lines around the sides of the circles for knurling.

3 Use a little water to adhere the knobs to the face of the radio under the display.

4 Re-roll the black fondant scraps to make a sheet $\frac{1}{4}$ in (6 mm) thick. Cut one 1-in (2.5-cm) circle and one $\frac{3}{4}$-in (1.8-cm) circle for the base of the antenna.

5 Adhere the two circles together with a little water, and

adhere them to the top right side of the radio. Insert a toothpick into the center.

6 Roll a marble-sized ball of blue fondant and insert onto the toothpick.

7 In a small bowl, mix together a small amount of black luster dust and vodka (it should be the consistency of thick gravy). Using a fine-tipped paint brush, paint the letters "FM" and your favorite radio station's number on the display.

8 In a small bowl, mix together some silver luster dust and vodka (it should be the consistency of thick gravy). Paint the knobs, speaker, antenna base, and exposed toothpick sliver. Leave the diagonal depressions on the speaker unpainted to create the illusion of depth.

British Punk

You've heard of an inner child. Well, some of us have an inner punk, a side of our personality that questions authority and chafes at convention—and likes to turn it up all the way up to eleven. You know who you are. Consider making differently colored mohawks in various styles, like big spikes or a giant fan, and add piercings. Even if *you* can't dress the part, your cakelet can.

Tools
6-cavity Wilton mini ball pan
The Necessities (pages 11–12)
Cake decorating tip #12

Ingredients
One 16-oz (455 g) box cake mix (any flavor)
  prepared, or batter for one 9-in (23-cm) cake
1 recipe Vanilla Frosting (page 17) or
  1 container store-bought frosting
10 oz (285 g) white fondant
  (see Resources, page 114)
4 oz (115 g) red fondant (if making the red
  mohawk cakelet)
4 oz (115 g) black fondant
2 oz (55 g) gray fondant
Electric blue gel food coloring (if making the
  blue mohawk cakelet)
Electric green gel food coloring (if making
  the green mohawk cakelet)
Silver luster dust
1 tablespoon vodka

Bake the cakes
1 Preheat oven to 350°F (180°C). Spray each of the mini ball cavities to be used with non-stick spray (you will need two mini ball cakes for one cakelet). Fill each cavity being used three-quarters full with batter. Bake for 10–12 minutes, or until the tops spring back when lightly pressed and

a toothpick inserted into the center comes out clean.

2 Allow cakes to cool for a few minutes in the pan. If the cakes are domed, use a serrated knife to trim the cakes until they are level (use the top of the pan as your guide). Run a knife around the edge to loosen the sides. Invert the cakes out of the pan onto a wire rack to finish cooling. When completely cool, wrap each in plastic wrap and freeze for at least two hours until cold and firm.

Prepare the cakelet
1 Remove cakes from the freezer and unwrap. Place each cake flat side down on parchment and cut away any hard edges.

2 Using a tapered angled spatula, apply a

layer of Vanilla Frosting to the bottom of one of the ball cakes. Adhere the bottom of another cake to it to form a sphere.

3 Cut away any rough edges where the two halves meet to make for a smooth seam. Cut out a wedge from the sphere so that the cakelet can sit flat.

4 Using a tapered angled spatula, crumb coat the cakelet with Vanilla Frosting. Use enough frosting so that the spatula doesn't come into direct contact with the cake. This will keep you from dislodging too many crumbs.

5 Repeat to form and coat the remaining cakelets.

Cover the cakelet
1 Dust a clean, dry work surface with cornstarch. Roll out $5\frac{1}{2}$ oz (160 g) of white fondant into a circle $\frac{1}{4}$ in (6 mm) thick and no larger than a dinner plate.

2 Slide your hand under the fondant, lift up, and gently lay it onto the cakelet and smooth it down and around the cake.

3 Cut away excess fondant with a pastry wheel.

4 Place in the refrigerator to chill for 30 minutes.

Finishing touches
Green mohawk
1 Tint 4 oz (115 g) of white fondant electric green. See the tinting instructions on page 16.

Level *Easy/Intermediate*
Batter yields enough cake for *3 cakelets*
Fondant quantity listed is suitable to complete *1 cakelet*

2 Remove the fondant covered cakelet from the refrigerator.

3 Dust a clean, dry work surface with cornstarch. Roll out the green fondant into a strip 4½ in (11.25 cm) long, ½ in (1.25 cm) wide and ¼ in (6 mm) thick.

4 Use scissors to cut a zig-zag along the edge to make the points of the mohawk. Twist each of the peaks of hair for a funky alternative look. ✺ Lightly brush water along the top of the cakelet and adhere the mohawk.

Red mohawk

1 Remove the fondant covered cakelet from the refrigerator.

2 Dust a clean, dry work surface with cornstarch. Roll out 4 oz (115 g) of red fondant into a strip 4½ in (11.25 cm) long, ½ in (1.25 cm) wide, and ¼ in (6 mm) thick.

3 Use an X-Acto knife to cut a fringe in the red fondant strip. Lightly brush water along the top of the cakelet and adhere the mohawk.

Blue mohawk

1 Tint 4 oz (115 g) of white fondant electric blue. See the tinting instructions on page 16.

2 Remove the fondant covered cakelet from the refrigerator.

3 Dust a clean, dry work surface with cornstarch. Roll out the blue fondant into a strip

4½ in (11.25 cm) long, ½ in (1.25 cm) wide, and ¼ in (6 mm) thick.

4 Use scissors to cut a zig-zag along the edge to make the points of the mohawk. Lightly brush water along the top of the cakelet and adhere the mohawk.

Black spiked band

1 Roll out 4 oz (115 g) of black fondant into a band approximately ¼ in (6 mm) thick ¾ in (1.8 cm) wide and 10 in (25.5 cm) long.

2 Apply water around the base of the cakelet and attach the black band to the cakelet, with the seam oriented toward the back.

3 Roll out gray fondant until it's ¼ in (6 mm) thick. Use the #12 decorating tip to cut out eight circles. Form half (or all) of these into spikes.

4 Apply water to the black band and adhere the circles/spikes, spacing them evenly apart.

5 Use a veining tool to imprint the center of each gray circle.

6 In a small bowl, mix together the silver luster dust and vodka until the mixture is the consistency of toothpaste.

7 Paint each of the circles/spikes silver.

Substitute Toppings

There have been many times when I've been in the middle of a cake design when I suddenly realize I don't have exactly what I need. Over the years, I've been able to improvise and have found that there are plenty of ingredients commonly found in your local grocery store that will do just fine in a pinch.

ROLLED FONDANT VS. TINTED FROSTING

If you love the cake designs in this book, but are not quite ready to commit to working with fondant, you can use tinted frosting and a tapered angled spatula to approximate the look of fondant. Be sure to first crumb coat your cakelet and let the icing set before you decorate. Placing your cakelet in the refrigerator will help quicken the process.

After your crumb coat of icing has set, remove your cakelet from the refrigerator. Use a piece of wax paper to gently smooth any bumps or cracks in the icing. When you are ready to decorate the cakelet with tinted frostings, be sure to keep a glass of warm water nearby for dipping your spatula. The heat from the water will heat the spatula, and this will help make your icing go on smoothly and cleanly.

NO FONDANT FOR DECORATIONS? NO PROBLEM!

You don't need to use fondant to create embellishments for your cakelets. The following candies can be used to create decorative flowers, shapes, borders, and even purse handles.

- Taffy
- Tootsie Rolls (warmed chocolate Tootsie Rolls are also a great substitution for chocolate fondant)
- Bubble gum
- Fruit roll-ups (fruit "leather")
- Caramels
- Airheads candies
- Candy clay

HELPFUL HINTS

Microwave the taffy or Tootsie Rolls at 5–10 second intervals until the candy is soft and malleable. As you are working with the candy it may begin to firm. It can be easily softened by reheating in the microwave.

To use Tootsie Rolls or taffy to cover your entire cakelet, unwrap multiple candies and knead them together after heating.

You will be able to use most flower cutters and even some texture sheets with these candy substitutes.

Appendix B
Presentation Tips

Cakelets are jaw-dropping, awe-inspiring treats—especially when given the pretty presentation they deserve. Not only are they wonderful individual desserts, they are also great gifts and party favors. Be sure you present them in a way that shows off your hard work and beautiful decorations.

CLEAR ACETATE BOXES: These are easy to find on the internet (see Resources, page 114), come in a variety of sizes and styles, and are easy to assemble. You can go with an elegant box rimmed in gold, or try something playful, like a Chinese takeout-

style box. The box I use the most is a 5-in (12.5-cm) square and 7 in (17.5 cm) tall with a gold bottom. It fits many of the designs in this book and it can be used standing up or on its side. Consider wrapping a ribbon around the box, adding a personalized label, or a simple peel-and-stick gift bow.

COVERED CAKE BOARD: Cover a cake board or cardboard cake circle with FDA-approved wrapping paper (look for food-safe paper at cake decorating shops). Place the cakelet on top. Set the board on top of a piece of clear polypropylene "cello" wrap and gather at the top. Using coordinating ribbon, tie a beautiful bow and trim any excess cello wrap.

CANDLE PEDESTALS AND PLATES: Go to your local craft chain and head straight to the candle aisle, where you will find an amazing variety of candle pedestals. The pedestals add height to your plated cakelet, making it a standout centerpiece, and they're just the right scale for your little cakes. Look for clear, scalloped, or decorative plates to set the cakelet on.

PARTY PRESENTATION: If you're planning on preparing dessert for a group, but have no time (or energy) to make multiple cakelets, the perfect solution is to make one centerpiece cakelet and

surround it with delicious (but simple!) color-coordinated cakelets. Use a candle pedestal for the cakelet centerpiece, and surround it with your adorable matching cupcakes. Your guests will be blown away by your amazing desserts and creative display, and the cakelet can be presented to the guest of honor as a special treat.

Appendix C
Resources

Here is a collection of some of the best places to buy the materials and tools called for in this book. A quick search on Amazon.com, eBay.com, or YouTube.com will usually find almost any tools, supplies, or tutorials you might need, but sometimes it's best to go straight to the source. The following represent but a small cross-section of the available products and information resources.

FONDANT, TOOLS, AND PANS

American Cake Decorating: www.americancakedecorating.com
Blue Lake Fox Cake Decorating: stores.ebay.com/bluelakefoxcakedecoratingtools
Durapak Supplies: www.durapak.net (clear acetate boxes—Durapak also has an ebay store that offers additional discounted products)
Earlene's Cakes: www.earlenescakes-store.com
Fondarific: www.fondarific.com
Global Sugar Art: www.globalsugarart.com
Satin Ice Fondant: www.satinice.com
Sugarcraft: www.sugarcraft.com
U.S. Cake Supply: www.uscake.com
Wilton: www.wilton.com

CLASSES, INFORMATION, BLOGS, AND INSPIRATION

Cake Journal: www.cakejournal.com
Cake Masters: www.cakemasters.com
Cake PLC: www.cakeplc.com
Cake Style TV: www.cakestyle.tv
Ceri Dz School of Cake Artistry: www.ceridz.co.uk
Craftsy: www.craftsy.com/cake-decorating
Cupcake Envy: www.shop.cupcakeenvy.com
Extra Icing: www.extraicing.co.uk
Learn Cake Decorating Online: www.learncakedecoratingonline.com
My Cake School: www.mycakeschool.com
Pretty Witty Cakes: www.prettywittycakes.co.uk
SugarEd Productions Sugar Art School: www.sugaredproductions.com
The Paul Bradford Sugarcraft School: www.designer-cakes.com
Wee Love Baking: www.weelovebaking.com
Wendy's Cake Space: www.wendyscakespace.com

T-Shirt template

Baby Onesie template

Mustache template

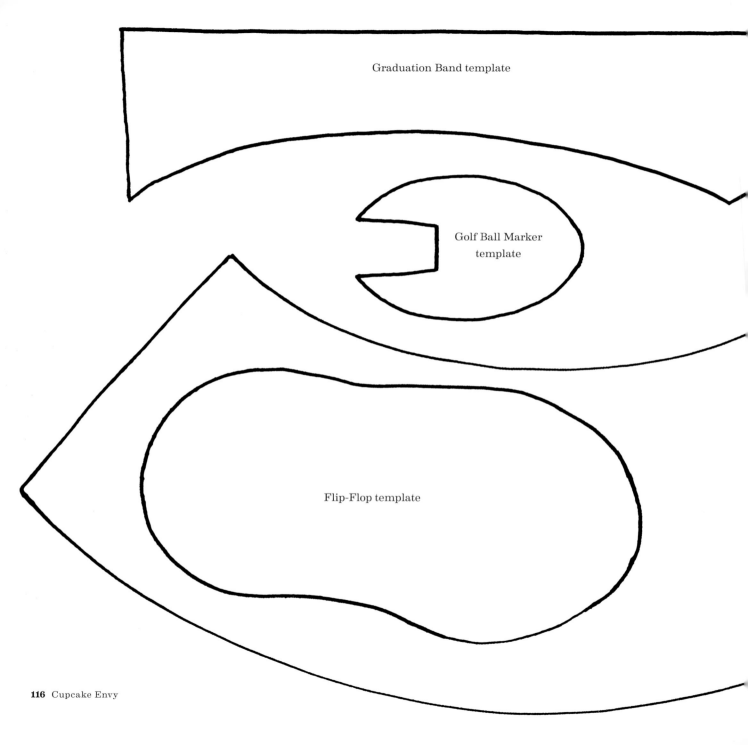

Graduation Band template

Golf Ball Marker
template

Flip-Flop template

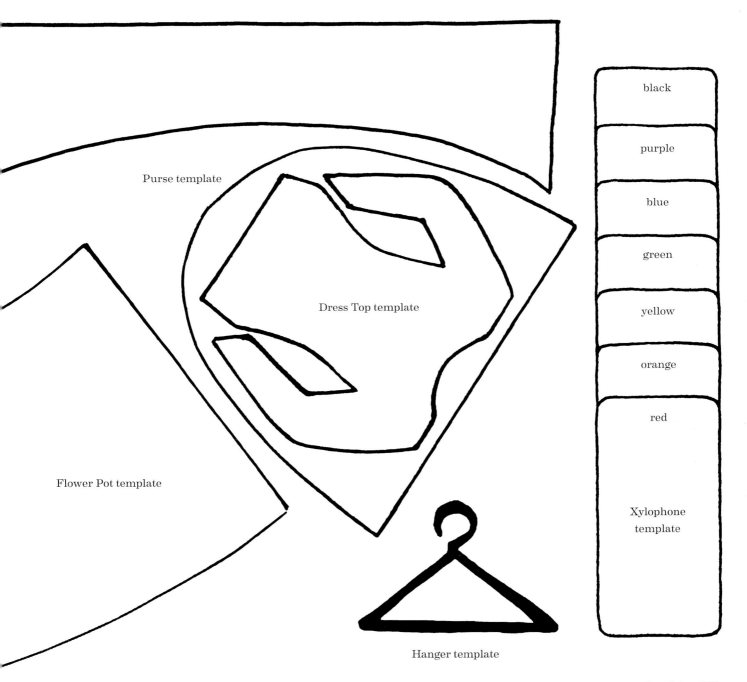

Purse template

Dress Top template

Flower Pot template

Hanger template

black

purple

blue

green

yellow

orange

red

Xylophone
template

Voodoo Doll template

Skirt Panel template

Coffee Cup Handle template

Teacup Handle template

Hook template

Acknowledgments

I would like to thank all of the talented cake artists and instructors I have had the pleasure of meeting and working with throughout my years with Cupcake Envy. The cake community is a very special group of passionate people with unique personalities, crazy talent, and a true love for creating. I always feel honored to be in their presence, as each cake artist is so accomplished in their craft and yet welcomed me with kindness and excitement into their world.

"Amy, you are very lucky that you found someone who is willing to put with you!" And boy, were they right. My husband Bill is my alter ego. Throughout the crazy ups and downs, he is by my side with kind words, love, and an indispensable sense of humor.

Thank you to my two boys: Ben and Sam, it was because of them that Cupcake Envy came to be. I have immense respect for them as individuals and the young men they are becoming. I love you, boys.

I would like to thank my mom and dad for their encouragement and support throughout the years. They taught me the value of hard work and perseverance. Though we live states away, they are always in my thoughts and I hope I have made them proud.

Thank you to my sister, Debbie, for being so much more than a sister. She's my best friend, my biggest cheerleader, and a pretty awesome cake class assistant. My sister's strength, guts, and unconditional love are traits I admire and value. I know I could not have done this without her.

I don't think a simple thank you would suffice for my dear friend and neighbor, Dana, who not only helped brand Cupcake Envy but has always given me sound advice, celebrated my successes, and helped me laugh off my failures. She will always be family to me.

Thank you to my agent, Stacey Glick, for her patience and commitment to my project. Thank you for believing in me.

Thank you to Tuttle Publishing for helping to bring my dreams of a book to fruition.

I'd like to thank Danielle Centoni for her expertise and guidance. This book would never have happened without her utmost commitment and knowledge. I have learned so much from you.

Writing this book has been such an amazing experience. So many wonderful friends and family helped me get to this point. I am sincerely grateful for the wonderful people in my life.

The Tuttle Story
Books to Span the East and West

Many people are surprised to learn that the world's largest publisher of books on Asia had its humble beginnings in the tiny American state of Vermont. The company's founder, Charles E. Tuttle, belonged to a New England family steeped in publishing.

Immediately after WWII, Tuttle served in Tokyo under General Douglas MacArthur and was tasked with reviving the Japanese publishing industry. He later founded the Charles E. Tuttle Publishing Company, which thrives today as one of the world's leading independent publishers.

Though a westerner, Tuttle was hugely instrumental in bringing a knowledge of Japan and Asia to a world hungry for information about the East. By the time of his death in 1993, Tuttle had published over 6,000 books on Asian culture, history and art—a legacy honored by the Japanese emperor with the "Order of the Sacred Treasure," the highest tribute Japan can bestow upon a non-Japanese.

With a backlist of 1,500 titles, Tuttle Publishing is more active today than at any time in its past—inspired by Charles Tuttle's core mission to publish fine books to span the East and West and provide a greater understanding of each.

Published by Tuttle Publishing, an imprint of
Periplus Editions (HK) Ltd

www.tuttlepublishing.com

Copyright © 2015 Amy Eilert

Library of Congress cataloging data in process

ISBN: 978-0-8048-4368-3

Distributed by

North America, Latin America & Europe
Tuttle Publishing
364 Innovation Drive
North Clarendon, VT 05759-9436 U.S.A.
Tel: (802) 773-8930; Fax: (802) 773-6993
info@tuttlepublishing.com
www.tuttlepublishing.com

Japan
Tuttle Publishing
Yaekari Building, 3rd Floor
5-4-12 Osaki
Shinagawa-ku
Tokyo 141-0032
Tel: (81) 3 5437-0171; Fax: (81) 3 5437-0755
sales@tuttle.co.jp
www.tuttle.co.jp

Asia Pacific
Berkeley Books Pte. Ltd.
61 Tai Seng Avenue, #02-12
Singapore 534167
Tel: (65) 6280-1330; Fax: (65) 6280-6290
inquiries@periplus.com.sg
www.periplus.com

First edition
18 17 16 15 14   10 9 8 7 6 5 4 3 2 1

Printed in Hong Kong   1410EP